Women, Hea
& Rep ction
Edited by erts

ISBN 0 7100 0703 5. Printed in Great Britain.

Cover illustration by Jo Nesbitt

Women, health and reproduction

Women, health and reproduction

Edited by
Helen Roberts

Routledge & Kegan Paul
London, Boston and Henley

First published in 1981
by Routledge & Kegan Paul Ltd
39 Store Street, London WC1E 7DD,
9 Park Street, Boston, Mass. 02108, USA, and
Broadway House, Newtown Road,
Henley-on-Thames, Oxon RG9 1EN
Set in IBM Baskerville, 11 on 12 pt
and printed in Great Britain by
Billing & Sons Ltd,
Guildford, London, Oxford & Worcester

British Library Cataloguing in Publication Data

Women, health and reproduction

1. Women – Sexual behaviour
I. Roberts, Helen
301.41'76'33 HQ29 80-49710

ISBN 0-7100-0703-5

Contents

Notes on contributors

Pauline Bart is a feminist sociologist employed by the Abraham Lincoln School of Medicine in the University of Illinois, Chicago. She has been active for some years in the women's movement in the USA and has done recent work on rape and abortion.

Katy Gardner studied psychology at university before changing to medicine. While at medical school, she became interested in women and health groups and self-help, and was involved in several such groups. In 1976, she joined the Communist Party and became involved in the women's movement at about the same time. She contributed to the *Women's Health Handbook* (Virago, 1976) and wrote *Why Suffer?* (Virago, 1979) with Lynda Birke. She is active in the abortion campaign and is currently a general practitioner running a Well Woman clinic in the practice.

Hilary Graham is a lecturer in applied social studies at the University of Bradford, and was previously involved in a major study at the University of York of the experience of early motherhood. She is a feminist and has two children.

Jalna Hanmer has written on women and violence and is active in Women's Aid and the British Sociological Association Women's Caucus. She is a lecturer in applied social studies at Bradford University and lives in Haworth with her son.

Ann Oakley is currently Honorary Research Officer at Bedford College, University of London, and Wellcome Research Fellow at the National Perinatal Epidemiology Unit, Churchill Hospital, Oxford, working on the history of antenatal care in Britain. She is a committed feminist and author of *Becoming a Mother* (Martin Robertson, 1979), *Women Confined: Towards a Sociology of Childbirth* (Martin Robertson, 1980) and *The Sociology of Housework* (Martin Robertson, 1974).

Jill Rakusen is a writer specialising in women's health issues and works for a Community Health Council in London. With Angela Phillips, she edited the British edition of *Our Bodies Ourselves* (1979). She has been active in the women's movement for many years.

Helen Roberts became involved in the women's movement in France in the late 1960s and has been mainly concerned with issues centring on women and health. She is Senior Researcher at Ilkley College and lives in the north of England.

Margaret Connor Versluysen teaches women's studies and the sociology of medicine and is writing a history of obstetricians. She read for a sociology degree after working for some years as a wife, mother and trained nurse, and has been active in feminist campaigns concerning health and reproduction since 1970. She lives in London with her son.

Gail Young qualified as a doctor in Edinburgh in 1973 and since then has worked in Scotland, Bristol and Newcastle. She has worked in various specialised areas as well as in general practice collecting an MRCP, DCH, and MRCGP on the way. She is about to go into general practice in Tyneside. She has been a feminist 'for ages, consciously only for 2-3 years' and dreams of the possibilities of setting up a non-sexist, democratically run Health (not Disease) Centre incorporating self-help and alternative therapies.

Introduction

In recent years and largely in response to the women's movement, there has been an upsurge of interest in the health of women and the control (or lack of it) that women have over their bodies and their lives. Largely outside the medical profession, but to a limited extent inside it, there has been a certain raising of consciousness on issues concerning women's health. Issues such as childbirth, contraception, abortion and artificial insemination now find a ready readership in newspapers and women's magazines as well as in textbooks and publications coming from the women's movement, and many of those writing can readily identify with the topics they are discussing.

In the past, there has often been a gap for women between 'legitimated knowledge' and personal experience. In such cases, it has frequently been assumed that it is the personal experiences which are mistaken. In this collection, there is an attempt to strike a balance between the personal and the political and to suggest that lived experiences are as legitimate as data as the articles we read in journals. All of the contributors have a personal as well as a professional interest in health and reproduction. This collection focuses on reproduction, presenting a wide spectrum of issues within a common feminist framework.

The first chapter by Helen Roberts on male hegemony in family planning looks in a general way at the structures through which male power operates in the field of birth control. This is followed by a careful historical overview by

Margaret Connor Versluysen of the way in which obstetricians began to take over the control of childbirth in the eighteenth century. Other chapters give evidence of the development of this encroachment whose thriving existence is witnessed by an editorial in the *British Medical Journal* (1977) entitled 'Helping Mothers to Love their Babies'.[1] In the third chapter, Hilary Graham and Ann Oakley draw on work from their childbirth studies to demonstrate the extent of differences between an obstetrician's view of childbirth and a mother's.

Jill Rakusen's chapter on a particular contraceptive, Depo-Provera, addresses a theme which recurs throughout the collection: the lack of access which women have to information on which to base decisions concerning their health. The two following chapters by Pauline Bart and Katy Gardner provide positive examples of strategies which have been shown to work in women's favour. Pauline Bart describes the successful operation of an illegal abortion collective run by and for women in Chicago, and Katy Gardner describes the work of Well Woman clinics and advocates their use as a force for change.

Gail Young, like Katy Gardner a general practitioner, discusses the inadequacies of medical education and training and suggests ways in which medical education could be improved. Finally, Jalna Hanmer's important chapter on sex predetermination, artificial insemination and the maintenance of male dominated culture explores technological developments in reproduction. She suggests that women need both to look at the development of technology and to extend their own personal control, warning that if they do not do so, these innovations could further reduce the control women have over their own bodies and sexuality. Recent reports[2] of a sperm bank for 'super babies' where women can be impregnated with the sperm of Nobel prize winners suggest that this concern is timely.

Although this collection documents the lack of power which women have in relation to their own bodies and their own fertility, it also suggests that there are areas where women could seize the means of reproduction, thus taking control of their bodies and their lives, and in this sense, contributors are attempting to link their professional work with their political practice.

Helen Roberts

Notes

1 *British Medical Journal*, 3 September 1977. Editorial: 'Helping Mothers to Love their Babies'.
2 'Super Babies Criticised', the *Guardian*, 3 March 1980.

Acknowledgments

This book would never have been started without encouragement from Carol Smart and Philippa Brewster and would never have been finished without help from May Douglas, Yvonne Edmondson, Helena Roberts and Dale Spender.

1

Male hegemony in family planning

Helen Roberts

It has frequently been argued that control of their own fertility is the largest single factor affecting the independence of women in the twentieth century. Other chapters in this collection document the dismal lack of such control in abortion, contraception and management of childbirth unless women are prepared to seize the means of reproduction themselves, as Pauline Bart suggests in her chapter. In this chapter, Helen Roberts looks at the sources of this lack of power and lack of control. In looking at the influence of the church, the state, the medical profession, research bodies, drug companies and the structure of personal relationships with men, she argues that there is a solid base of male power in these areas which must be attacked if women are to gain control. Although there is a very real sense in which contraception is the responsibility *of women, they have limited rights, limited control of the relevant technology, and limited access, as Jill Rakusen shows, to the information needed to make an informed choice.*

Because the dominant institutions which control contraception from the point of production to the point of access are not areas where women have power, women are operating within structures which are not of their own making. As Zoë Fairbairns's novel Benefits *(1979) indicates, there could well be startling effects if women were to have real power over their own fertility. Paradoxically, in Britain at least, a certain amount of the* delivery *of contraceptive provision is in female hands, but in common with education at the primary level, the fact that provision at the shop floor is in female hands does not affect the fact that the concentration of power does not rest with women. Gail Young and Katy Gardner show in their chapters the contradictions of working as both feminists and doctors. This chapter indicates that such contradictions are deep seated, and in the area of production and reproduction, range from the highest level of policy-making to the intimacy of personal relationships.*

> 'Don't fancy the cap, I don't fancy mucking about with that. I don't fancy Durex, they've given us loads, we've got loads upstairs, we can't give 'em away, can we? Gave us one and a half dozen and we haven't used one. Don't fancy Durex at all, I think they're horrible . . . you know, I hate this idea of stop, hang on, you know, this sort of thing. And what else is there? I didn't fancy the pill again. I've never been right, have I, since I went on the pill?'[1]

Family planning is a world-wide institution dominated by the interests of males. In this chapter, I look at what these areas of male dominance are, what their implications are for research and policy, and above all what their implications are for women in their daily lives. For, as the above quotation shows, neither rubber technology nor drug technology have succeeded in identifying contraceptive techniques which are both safe and acceptable to the consumer. Much of the work on family planning (and Jill Rakusen's chapter is an example of this) points to cultural imperialism and the exploitation of poor women and black women. Such women are obviously in a particularly disadvantaged position, but contraception remains an area where all heterosexual women are disadvantaged by a limited choice. Either they can 'choose' systemic methods like the contraceptive pill or Depo-Provera, which may be relatively 'safe' as contraceptives but which have been shown to have dangers in terms of general health, or they can choose an 'invasive' contraceptive such as the intra-uterine device which can also endanger their health. Barrier methods are frequently unacceptable to women for other reasons, as the above extract from an interview shows.

The very use of the term 'family planning' as a euphemism for birth control or contraception indicates a particular construction on heterosexual sexuality, with primacy given to reproductive functions within the family. This is well indicated in a booklet published by the International Planned Parenthood Federation in 1975 to mark International Women's Year (IPPF, 1975, p. 6):

> Marriage and family life are very important to the majority of women in the world, and even given economic independence it is unrealistic to think that a significant number of women would choose to remain single. Marriage offers affection, physical security, children and often a higher standard of living than a woman could provide for herself.

Moral imperatives and assumptions about marriage and the family have always formed a backdrop to planning and provision of contraception and abortion, and clearly continue to do so.

Perhaps the most invasive form of male control on an ideological level is the control by the church: 'The Catholics have agents in the condom factories – they prick one in every fifty rubbers with a pin with the Pope's head on it' (Weldon, 1973 p. 18). This (presumably) fictitious account from *Down Among the Women* points to the particular form of Russian roulette advocated by a church which permits only the use of an inadequate and unreliable rhythm method. Although as Caldwell (1978) shows, pronouncements coming from the Pope in the 1960s tended to place a greater emphasis than before on the loving and sharing aspects of marriage, the basic tenets of *Casti conubii*, the papal encyclical of 1930, remain largely unchallenged. This encyclical (Caldwell, p. 72; quotations from *Casti conubii*, p. 37):

> reiterated the importance of the gender based hierarchy within the family and the tasks assigned to the partners on the basis of it. It argued against the movement of women towards emancipation on the grounds that this would be unnatural and constitute a perversion of family life, and would even result in 'crime' because 'it would free the wife from the domestic cares of children and family, enabling her to the neglect of these, to follow her own bent, and engage in business and even public affairs.'

Such views have a long history within the Christian church. McLaughlin (1974, pp. 222-3), writing on women in medieval theology, points out that:

> It must be remembered that the woman, defined with reference to her ultimate reason for being as an aid in reproduction, is more essentially involved in marriage than is the male. Her position in the marriage relationship is however, subordinate and auxiliary . . . biologically, the woman assumes a passive and auxiliary role in conformity with the inferiority of her body. Thomas grounds this view in Aristotelian physiology, in which the active principle of procreation is carried wholly by the male sperm containing the human embryo *in potentia* which needs only the mother's 'inner space' for growth and nourishment. The sex act performed with the intention to prohibit conception is sinful, not because the woman violates her potentiality as mother but because the teleology of the male sperm is violated.

Evidence from women fitted with intra-uterine devices indicates the human cost of wrestling with these beliefs. One woman fitted with an IUD returned to the clinic after three months with no complaints, but 'no pregnancy for past year so now feels guilty'. Another woman, Irish like the first, and with seven children while she herself was still under the age of thirty, had her coil removed after two months, saying that she would rather have an eighth child than any form of contraception. A third had her device removed after three months because of a 'moral problem', and a fourth had hers removed after a similar period of time because she was 'tormented psychologically'. It is interesting to note that the Catholic view on abortion has not been quite as constant as we sometimes believe. Roberts (1976, p. 28) points out that:

> In the 1200s the Catholic male clergy considered abortion acceptable before the foetus moved. In 1588 by male papal decree, all abortions were murder. Three years later, another male papal decree reversed this position, establishing a forty day limitation. That ruling lasted until 1869 when male clerics again prohibited abortion.

Linked with the church as a male-dominated interest group in the area of family planning is the state. It is not for nothing that the abortion slogan for feminists, so often resurrected as yet another assault is made on the abortion laws is:

> Not the Church
> Not the State
> Women shall decide our fate

But as Dowse and Peel (1965, p. 179) point out, the whole area of contraception and birth control has never been a major political issue in the UK.

> None of the major political parties displayed any real enthusiasm in promoting contraception although considerable political and social pressure for reform was organised inside the Labour Party. Within the Conservative Party there was a considerable measure of inchoate

sympathy with those who demanded birth control as a public service, but in neither party was the leadership keen to champion birth control – a potential vote loser.

Nevertheless, even in Britain (which has never had a significant population 'problem') there has been a state interest in both contraception and abortion, although it appears that it has never been intended by Parliament in any of its legislation, particularly on abortion, that women should have freedom of choice in the matter. There is some reason for feminists to feel that little progress has been made in the matter of choice, particularly in the area of a woman's right to 'choose', if necessary, an abortion. This particular right has involved a constant struggle even to remain in the same place.

Such struggles have a long history. In July 1924, Miss Jewson MP asked the appropriate minister whether he was aware that many working-class women attending welfare centres were unfit to bear and bring up healthy children, that their doctors knew this, and yet remained unable to give the sort of information which any upper- or middle-class woman could obtain from a private doctor. At that time (and for some time afterwards) local authority clinics providing such information were under threat of having their grants withdrawn if they offered birth control advice to mothers. Two years after Miss Jewson's question, in 1926, the Local Authorities Birth Control (Enabling) Bill was introduced under the ten-minute rule, and solidly defeated. One of those successfully opposing the bill suggested that

> a Bountiful Creator has provided ample resources for all. . . . These moral instincts and these religious prejudices, call them what you will, are after all the purest, the finest, the most powerful and the most potent influences in the uplift of mankind; . . . if we chose to defy them or ignore them we do so at our peril and at the peril of the state.

Such historical gems merely serve as grim reminders of the slow progress in the fight for women to control their own fertility.

In countries with a greater state interest in population in relation to the work force, state intervention can have an even more dire effect on a woman's right to control her own fertility. The availability, and then the withdrawal, of abortion rights for instance, can very effectively alter the birth rate. Hilda Scott (1978) points out that the liberalised abortion laws adopted by the governments of Eastern Europe in the mid-1950s (with the exception of the German Democratic Republic) rendered abortion a favoured method of birth control. This had a dramatic effect on the population, so that by the mid to late 1960s, Bulgaria, Poland, Romania, Hungary and Czechoslovakia were no longer reproducing their populations. Scott points to the consequences of this (Scott, 1978, p. 193):

> Gynaecologists began publishing evidence, in Hungary and Czechoslovakia particularly, purporting to show that legally induced abortion impaired women's ability to conceive and to carry future wanted pregnancies to term . . . information on 'maternal deprivation' was belatedly reaching Eastern Europe from Western sources and dispelling some of the faith in collective child care . . . it was not long before the advisability of keeping a child at home for the first two or three years emerged as scientific fact, and woman's 'natural role as mother and guardian of the hearth' was discovered to be her primary role under socialism too.

The effect of all this was a modification of the right to abortion in four countries, child care allowances to enable mothers in Hungary and Czechoslovakia to remain at home, and, since 1973, a policy of 'more children in every Bulgarian family'. According to this policy, writes Scott, 'Motherhood is not only of "vital importance for society", it is "essential" for women's "own self confidence and happiness" ' (ibid., p. 194).

As a character in Zoë Fairbairns's novel *Benefits* suggests, 'Population is the louse in the ointment of planning' (p. 199).

A third area of male domination of birth control is that of the medical establishment, and linked directly and indirectly with this are research bodies and drug companies (which frequently provide funds for research). In addition, the policies of the Health Education Council in Britain appear to be very much dominated by the medical model (Weldon, 1973, p. 18):

> There is a birth control clinic down in the slums. You have to pretend to be married. They ask you how often you have intercourse – be prepared. They say it's for their statistics, but it's probably just to catch you out.

Analysis of the distribution of power in the medical profession and its concentration in male hands has come largely from feminists. Scully and Bart's (1973) account of the blatant sexism of gynaecology textbooks in use in medical schools revealed that such texts expressed traditional attitudes about female sexuality. Very much linked to an understanding of medicine as an institution of social control in the area of contraception as in other areas is the pronounced male domination within the profession. The title of Becker and his associates' classic (1961) in the field of medical education, *Boys in White: Student Culture in Medical School*, is extremely revealing, although recently there has been more interest taken in the training of women doctors. As Bewley and Bewley (1975) have pointed out in the *Lancet*, the rate at which women doctors drop out as a result of family obligations is not significantly higher than the rate for men dropping out through alcoholism, drug addiction, emigration, removal from the medical register and so on.

In spite of the increase in the number of women qualifying as doctors however, high status posts both in practice and research remain on the whole the province of men, and it should not be forgotten that, as Gail Young shows, there is a certain pressure on the non-conforming feminist or socialist doctor to adopt the dominant ideology of the profession. Certainly, there is some reason to believe that in the past at least, women doctors have often had to be more 'one of the boys' than the boys themselves in order to succeed.

A phenomenon common to all the professions is the tendency to withhold information from potential consumers and then to accuse those consumers of ignorance. Nowhere is this more evident than in the medical profession. Doctors will tell with barely suppressed amazement of women who do not know the size or location of their own uterus, or women who have bizarre ideas about the workings of their own bodies. But how *would* they know? Certainly not through any freely available information offered them by the medical profession. Recent years have seen a significant growth in the self-help health movement for women, and Bart's chapter describes one of the forms that this has taken. Books such as *Our Bodies Ourselves* (Boston Women's Health Book Collective, 1976; Phillips and Rakusen, 1978) and *The New Women's Health Handbook* (Mackeith, 1978), have provided women with information which would otherwise be inaccessible to them, and on an even more influential if less radical level, the health and medical pages of popular womens' magazines are providing women with information about their bodies and their health rights. Increases in the medical management of childbirth have led to a backlash from women who might, in other circumstances, not be the first to criticise the medical profession. It should be said that this challenge to medical authority, although it may represent a population of more informed patients, does not appear to be welcomed with open arms by the medical profession. Some doctors talk of a new generation of 'nosey' women who want details of everything that is happening to their bodies. Others are horrified at the idea of a woman inserting a speculum into her own vagina to examine her cervix. Of course, the speculum used in the home may well not be a sterilised instrument, but then neither, on the whole, is the penis.

Traditional 'family planning' textbooks offer little comfort for those wanting a change in attitudes at the sharp end of the service. One textbook (Pollock, 1966) suggests: 'Intrauterine devices are particularly useful for women of low intelligence . . . who are incapable of using any other method of birth control effectively; the contraceptive precautions are entirely out of their hands' (p. 6). She goes on: 'when the woman complains her enjoyment (is) unsatisfactory, the *frigidity* must be examined' (p. 124, my emphasis). So long as the medical profession retains control of the effective (though one cannot say 'safe') methods of birth control, women must continue to challenge its authority and seek access to information.

In the UK the Health Education Council, although not actually a part of the medical establishment, appears to be significantly influenced by a medical person's (rather than, for instance, a patient's) view of the world. Since it is the patient, or the potential patient, whom the council seeks to influence, this is unfortunate. In looking at much of the advertising of the Council, one can discern a certain patronising attitude, not unknown within the medical profession. One colourful advertisement strategically placed in women's magazines asked: 'How can another woman make you pregnant?' The answer was that she could make you pregnant by giving you advice and that the best and most reliable advice comes from your doctor. Of course, given the lack of access which women have to such information as is available on contraceptives, there is probably a sense in which this is true. What is objectionable is that it devalues the traditional advice passed from one woman to another, and lends credence to the view that 'old wives' tales' are a danger rather than valuable tales of experience and a basis for what Pauline Bart would call 'the body of knowledge on the knowledge of bodies'.[2] Other health education literature advises women through expensive advertisements that they should not smoke during pregnancy and that they should remember to attend the antenatal clinic as soon as possible. Such advertisements appear to be based on the view that if only the consumer 'knows' what she 'ought' to be doing the battle is half won. There is unlikely to be a substantial body of women in the UK who do not know of the existence of antenatal clinics. There is a substantial body of women who do know of their existence but are unwilling or unable to travel over the town by public transport with younger children in tow, who cannot afford the long waits, who do not like sitting around with their knickers off, or who, since they have never had the purpose of their visits and their tests fully explained to them, believe that there is none. Other women complain that they are treated as if on a conveyor belt, and that their questions go unanswered (and sometimes unasked too, since they are so intimidated). Hilary Graham and Ann Oakley give examples in their chapter of these differing perceptions, and one might well argue that the Health Education Council should be *listening* to the women rather than talking to them. The top echelons of the Health Education Council are, as one would expect, male dominated, and there would often seem to be little link between some of the research they fund and their education campaigns in the press. One might suggest that research on motherhood by Hilary Graham and Lorna McKee (Graham, 1976a; 1976b; 1977a; 1977b), to give one example of work funded by the Health Education Council, might profitably influence future campaigns in the area of antenatal care, childbirth and the post-natal period.

Although there is a certain amount of non-commercial research funding for medicine in the UK, of necessity a good deal of research into contraceptives and contraceptive technology is funded directly or indirectly by drug companies. There is, of course, an enormous potential market. To take the contraceptive pill as an example, one can imagine the income derived from millions of healthy women swallowing a pill for 21 days out of every 28. The politics of research funding is a difficult area, and there is sometimes a persuasive case for the end justifying the means. On the whole, however, the relationship between capital and care is a difficult one as Rakusen shows. It is important to bear in mind that contraceptive technology, by and large, is in the hands of multi-national corporations and not the corner chemist.

The advertisements for oral contraceptives, as Stimson's work (1975) shows so well, tend to present a particular stereotype of women, and frequently a highly romantic and misleading one. Since the contraceptive pill cannot be bought over the counter, it is the doctors who are exposed to romantic stereotypes of their female patients in this context (and other stereotypes in other contexts such as in the marketing of tranquillisers and anti-depressants). This is hardly a course to facilitate a realistic relationship between a male doctor and his female patient, and although doctors may well argue that they remain unaffected by such advertisements, the drug companies, spending vast sums of money each year, clearly believe otherwise.

It has been argued that the concern that women feel in taking oral contraceptives is misplaced and that these drugs are the 'most tested'. Perhaps this is the case, but this view fails to recognise the fact that oral contraceptives are unique in their position as drugs taken on virtually a daily basis by large numbers of healthy women over many years. There are of course large numbers of women doctors who themselves use oral contraceptives, but it might be useful to speculate how the world of contraception would look if women were the manufacturers, distributors and prime researchers in birth control as well as the consumers. Belita Cowan's spoof abstract (1980) on the 'intrapenal device' is instructive in this context. Describing a device pushed into the scrotum in much the same way as the intra-uterine device is inserted into the uterus, she points out that occasional perforation is unimportant since the male has few nerve endings in this area. Trials are described as having taken place on whales which were 'eminently satisfactory to the female whale since it doesn't interfere with her rutting pleasure'. Of trials on human males, only relatively small numbers had developed scrotal infection, swelling of the tissues, cancer of the testicles or depression. Other symptoms were 'merely indications that the man's body had not yet adjusted to the device'. As in other areas where roles are reversed, such a technique serves to bring home to us the assumptions that underlie descriptions of side effects in women users.

At a different level, I have described elsewhere (Roberts, 1979) the sexist underpinnings of assumptions concerning social class in family planning research. As Kingsley and McEwan (1978, p. 353) point out in their discussion of social class and contraception:

> Those who are married, or married but separated, are assigned by the occupation of their husbands; those who are single, widowed or divorced are assigned by virtue of their own occupation if gainfully employed and are not classifiable if their work is solely in the home.

The classification they describe is a relatively advanced one. In some classificatory schemes, women, even when gainfully employed, are assigned to their father's social class if single, their deceased husband's if a widow and their ex-husband's if divorced. If we see social class as being a relevant index at all in examining the use and provision of contraception (and there is some evidence that social class is a good deal more relevant than some of the other data collected) then there would seem to be a fair case for collecting more reliable information about the women themselves. Literature in this area demonstrates a distribution of and 'demand' for contraceptive methods along social class lines, but it is difficult to know quite what this means when we are looking at the social class of the husband rather than the wife. Of course, it is not only in family planning research that this occurs. In Britain, the following somewhat idiosyncratic instructions are given to interviewers by the Office of Population, Censuses and Surveys (Atkinson, 1971, pp. 116-19):

> In each household, there can be only one head of household (HOH) and one housewife. . . . So long as the husband is resident he takes precedence over the wife in being HOH. This means if you have a married couple living together, even if the wife owns the property or has her name on the rent book, you count her husband as the HOH. . . . When two persons of different sex have an equal claim to be HOH, i.e. you are told ownership is joint, then you take the male of the two to be HOH. . . . If two persons of different sex share the housekeeping duties EQUALLY, then the woman is the housewife, though a man CAN be the housewife if he carries out MOST of the domestic duties, or is responsible for seeing that a paid servant does so.

If women were to hold the purse-strings in public expenditure in this kind of work, would such misapprehensions continue? To suggest that the *status quo* of male hegemony in this area affects the information we have available to us, the access we have to this information, the technology we have available and the delivery of the service, is not to suggest a crude male conspiracy. It is merely to suggest that the direct consumers of the service, in this case women, could well lay claim to a different approach.

Male hegemony in family planning is not however confined to the structural level. As well as the structural manifestations of power through the church, the state, the medical establishment and drug companies, there are manifestations of personal power through the structure of relationships between women and men. As Sheila Rowbotham (1973) has pointed out: 'The relationship of man to woman is like no other relationship of oppressor to oppressed. It is far more delicate, far more complex. . . . It is a rather gentle tyranny. We are subdued at the very moment of intimacy' (p. 34). But however delicate and gentle, the power relationship is a real one. There has been a long history of the 'duty' of a wife to provide her husband with a son, and of the necessity to carry on the family name. Much of the literature on contraceptive methods for women emphasises that such methods should also be 'acceptable' to the men, and quotations from Hilary Graham and Lorna McKee's pregnancy and motherhood survey[3] demonstrate that a concern with the needs of the male is not misplaced:

> 'I want to go back on the pill, but me husband won't let me. It took me quite a long time to catch on (i.e., get pregnant) . . . that's why he won't let me. I could go on it, I don't want one till he's about three – if ever. But he thinks it takes too long when you come off, that's why he won't let me. . . .'

The husband of another respondent gives his views on a male method:

> 'She wanted me to have the knife, but I'm not too willing. . . . I'm not keen on that vasectomy. No, I know about three blokes that's had it done and two out of three haven't been very pleasant with it. . . . One bloke couldn't walk . . . to me it isn't final yet. They don't know. I mean it's like landing rockets on t'moon. It's alright, they've landed them at one side and they ain't

found nowt. But if they land them at t'other they might get devoured by summat. They don't know. I'd rather it was proved.'

Such a view illustrates a delicate balance of power. Just as men do not normally have to wonder whether to have a child or continue their career – both are normally possible – a man is not normally under immediate and urgent pressure to accept a method of birth control with which he is not happy. Heterosexual women on the whole do not have this choice; for them it is not possible to say, 'I'd rather it was proved.'

In English law, a woman does not need the consent of her husband to have contraception although as Stimson and Stimson (1980) point out, some family planning groups and doctors take the extremely cautious approach that the permission of the husband is required, and certainly the informal control which individual husbands exercise over individual wives in this matter appears to be substantial.

Thus men, without actually having the power to reproduce themselves, have a very direct power over the means of reproduction. It is men who control the church and the state, the medical establishment is male dominated as are the drug companies, men do (or at least design) the bulk of the research and women are made to fit into male-defined categories. It is thus important that women start to take control at every level. Pauline Bart shows that women can learn appropriate skills and do not merely have to receive them, Katy Gardner points to an increased access to knowledge through Well Woman clinics and Jalna Hanmer describes an initiative in artificial insemination taken by one group of women. We should not be surprised to see that if men look at reproduction, they will determine what is significant in their own terms, and will not always make decisions which are in the best interests of women. In order to make the best of the available choices, and indeed expand the choices available, women must, in Bart's terms, seize the means of reproduction at every level.

Notes

1 This and subsequent quotations on contraception are taken from a survey of pregnancy and motherhood directed by Professor Laurie Taylor and undertaken by Hilary Graham and Lorna McKee in the Institute of Social and Economic Research, University of York. This research was funded by the Health Education Council.

2 Pauline Bart, who would undoubtedly have had a career as a headline writer had she not become an academic, originally suggested this phrase as a title for the present collection.

3 Graham and McKee, op. cit. (see note 1 above).

References

Atkinson, J. (1971), *A Handbook for Interviewers* (produced for OPCS Survey Division), HMSO, London.

Becker, H., Geer, B., Hughes, E.C., and Strauss, A. (1961), *Boys in White: Student Culture in Medical School*, University of Chicago Press.

Bewley, B.R., and Bewley, T.H. (1975), 'Hospital Doctors' Career Structure and Misuse of Medical Womanpower', the *Lancet*, 2, 9 August, pp. 270-2.

Boston Women's Health Book Collective (1976), *Our Bodies Ourselves*, Simon & Schuster, New York.

Caldwell, L. (1978), 'Church, State and Family, the Women's Movement in Italy', in Annette Kuhn and Ann Marie Wolpe (eds), *Feminism and Materialism*, Routledge & Kegan Paul, London.

Casti conubii (1930), English translation published by Catholic Truth Society, London, 1965.

Cowan, B. (1980), 'Breakthrough in Male Contraception', *Spare Rib*, April, Issue 93, p. 9 (reprinted from *East Bay Men's Centre Newsletter* and *The Periodical Lunch*, Ann Arbor, Michigan).

Dowse, R., and Peel, J. (1965), 'The Politics of Birth Control', *Political Studies*, vol. 13, no. 2, pp. 179-97.

Fairbairns, Z. (1979), *Benefits*, Virago, London.

Graham, H. (1976a), 'The Social Image of Pregnancy: Pregnancy as a Spirit Possession', *Sociological Review*, vol. 32, pp. 291-308.

Graham, H. (1976b), 'Smoking in Pregnancy: the Attitudes of Expectant Mothers', *Social Science and Medicine*, vol. 10, pp. 399-405.

Graham, H. (1977a), 'Images of Pregnancy in Antenatal Literature', in R. Dingwall, C. Heath, M. Reid, and M. Stacey (eds), *Health Care and Health Knowledge*, Croom Helm, London, pp. 13-38.

Graham, H. (1977b), 'Women's Attitudes to Conception and Pregnancy', in R. Chester and J. Peel (eds), *Equalities and Inequalities in Family Life*, Academic Press, London.

International Planned Parenthood Federation (1975), *Half of Humanity*, IPPF, London.
Kingsley, S., and McEwan, J. (1978), 'Social Class for Women of Differing Marital Status', *Journal of Biosocial Science*, vol. 10, pp. 353-9.
Mackeith, N. (ed) (1978), *The New Women's Health Handbook*, Virago, London.
McLaughlin, E. C. (1974), 'Equality of Souls, Inequality of Sexes: Women in Medieval Theology', in R. Radford Ruether (ed.), *Religion and Sexism*, Simon & Schuster, New York.
Phillips, A., and Rakusen, J. (1979), *Our Bodies Ourselves*, Penguin, Harmondsworth.
Pollock, M. (1966), *Family Planning*, Ballière, London.
Roberts, H. (1979), 'Women, Social Class and IUD Use' *Women's Studies International Quarterly*, vol. 1, no. 2, pp. 49-56.
Roberts, J. (1976), *Intellectual Sexism; A New Woman, a New Reality*, David McKay, New York.
Rowbotham, S. (1973), *Women's Consciousness, Man's World*, Penguin, Harmondsworth.
Scott, H. (1978), 'Eastern European Women in Theory and Practice', *Women's Studies International Quarterly*, vol. 1, no. 2, pp. 189-99.
Scully, D., and Bart, P. (1973), 'A Funny Thing Happened to me on the Way to the Orifice', *American Journal of Sociology*, vol. 78, pp. 1045-9.
Stimson, G. (1975), 'Women in a Doctored World', *New Society*, 1 May, pp. 265-7.
Stimson, G., and Stimson, C. (1980), *Health Rights Handbook*, Penguin, Harmondsworth.
Weldon, F. (1973), *Down Among the Women*, Penguin, Harmondsworth.

2

Midwives, medical men and 'poor women labouring of child': lying-in hospitals in eighteenth-century London[1]

Margaret Connor Versluysen

Hilary Graham and Ann Oakley writing on the different perspectives on childbirth of obstetricians and mothers reveal contemporary problems in the management of childbirth. Margaret Versluysen, in this chapter on lying-in hospitals, gives a background to the way in which childbirth became classified as a 'problem' in which medical men could and should intervene, as and when they thought appropriate.

Versluysen's discussion highlights the apparent contradiction that you could not be a lying-in patient if you were sick. Not only did women have to be healthy to fulfil the medical definition of patient, they had to be morally healthy as well. 'Only two lying-in institutions,' she points out, 'the General Lying In and Queen Charlotte's, admitted unmarried mothers, and then only in the first pregnancy so as not "to encourage vice".'

What then was the motive for taking moral, healthy, normal, women patients under the control of doctors? It seems that the only basis was just that: control. *This was an area in which male control over women could be exerted profitably. As Versluysen demonstrates, childbirth became a medical concern in the second half of the seventeenth century because it afforded medical men the opportunity to dominate the formerly female field of midwifery and to subordinate female midwives and patients to medical authority. As the chapter shows, these objectives were behind the extension of medical control to include the establishment of maternity hospitals in the eighteenth century. It suggests that the London lying-in hospitals provide not only a case study of entrepreneurial medical professionalism but also the exercise of male dominance over women's work as midwives.*

In England, before the eighteenth century, home-birth was the norm in all social classes, and although it is possible that some medieval hospices may have received pregnant women, these institutions were destroyed in the Reformation, and the surviving London foundations, St Bartholomew's and St Thomas's, did not accept maternity cases until the latter half of the nineteenth century (Holland, 1954). Some maternity hospitals were opened on the continent in the sixteenth and seventeenth centuries (Gunn, 1964, p. 101), but similar institutions did not appear in England until the mid-eighteenth century. Between 1739 and 1765 two lying-in wards and four separate lying-in hospitals were created in London for 'taking care of poor women labouring of child', followed by six provincial hospitals in the period up to 1800.[2] The London lying-in hospitals set an important precedent in the history of childbirth since they represented the first successful attempt in this country to bring parturition under professional medical management in a secular institutional setting and provided a model for later hospital development. The lying-in hospitals only accounted for a fraction of the working-class birth rate in the capital[3] and from the 1770s a large number of outdoor lying-in charities were founded all over the country.[4] These domiciliary charities were much cheaper than hospitals, nevertheless another twenty-five charitable lying-in hospitals were built before 1921 (Gunn, 1964), whilst throughout this period maternity beds proliferated in the Poor Law sector (Berkeley, 1929). From 1921 the provision of maternity beds rapidly accelerated. After the Second World War, the middle classes began to make extensive use of maternity hospitals and today hospital delivery has become the typical childbirth style for all sections of society.

The original London lying-in hospitals have received little detailed treatment from historians, and even a recent history of midwifery devotes little more than cursory attention to these innovatory institutions, except in so far as they were willing to provide training for midwives (Donnison, 1977). This chapter outlines the reasons for the provision of secular maternal hospitals in this period, for whom, and for what reasons.

A recent study of eighteenth-century voluntary hospitals as a social movement for the care of the acutely sick poor treats the lying-in foundations as a specialised facet of that movement (Woodward, 1974). But the lying-in hospitals have a separate specialist history and do not fit neatly into the general explanatory schema of the voluntary hospital movement. Despite the therapeutic limitations of eighteenth-century medicine, the character of the hospital was changing rapidly in this period and a recognisably modern social institution was emerging. The charitable ethos of the medieval hospice with its open-door policy for all categories of the needy and disabled was rejected in favour of a highly selective admissions policy which redesignated the hospital as a specifically medical centre for the treatment of illness. Whilst this was an optimistic medical ideal for the time, it meant that voluntary hospitals, although charitably founded, rejected the chronically ill and many in need of care (Woodward, 1974, p. 45), in favour of certain categories of the working-class sick who were potentially curable. The management of the acutely ill therefore became the central function of the eighteenth-century hospital, and it is necessary to ask why this new type of institutional care was thought appropriate for healthy young parturient women, who, even if debilitated by poverty, were not presenting any pathology but had reached the usual outcome of pregnancy, i.e. childbirth. Although birth can have pathological consequences, it is nevertheless a natural physiological condition, and hospital records for the period plainly show that patients suffering from any recognisable complicating conditions, especially infections, were refused admission. Aside from the onset of labour, the main requirements for admission to a lying-in hospital were proven poverty, a letter of recommendation from a hospital subscriber, proof of settlement in the parish in which the hospital was situated, together with an affidavit of marital status. Only two of the lying-in institutions, the General Lying In and Queen Charlotte's, admitted unmarried mothers, and then only in the first pregnancy, so as not 'to encourage vice'. Since, in modern times, the possibility of complications has often been used as a rationale for hospitalisation, it might be assumed that patients in lying-in hospitals were selected according to some identification of specific obstetric risk. But systematic antenatal care was non-existent in the eighteenth century and the selection of high-risk cases would therefore have been difficult, if not impossible.

Further, the statistical incidence of complications in childbirth has often been exaggerated by doctors, as the discussion below on the use of forceps will show. Since the hospital as an institution implicitly redefined birth as a state akin to acute illness although its patients were in the natural condition of pregnancy and were 'healthy', it might be assumed that some contemporaneous developments in midwifery techniques or medical therapy were responsible for a new institutional approach to birth. But this does not seem to have been so: indeed, despite the popularisation of the obstetric forceps, technical developments appear to have provided neither the rationale nor the motivation for the foundation of lying-in hospitals. Further, aside from slight hygienic improvements, little could be done in the eighteenth century to improve the outcome of childbirth for either mother or child (McKeown and Brown, 1955; Gilliatt, 1954; Kerr, 1954). Infant mortality was very high and exacerbated by hospital cross-infection.

Medicine was virtually powerless in the face of the principal complications which caused maternal death. Toxaemias of pregnancy, sepsis and haemorrhage, the principal maternal killers, were not brought under effective medical control until the 1930s with the advent of antenatal care, chemotherapy and blood transfusion. Indeed the national maternal death rate, first computed in 1835, remained at an almost constant high until 1935 (Gilliatt, 1954). It was the desire to establish male control rather than therapeutic advances in medicine that provided the impetus for the creation of maternity hospitals.

This analysis is only comprehensible if brief reference is made to the prior history of English midwifery. It will show that progressive male medical intrusion into birth management provoked hostile reactions from female midwives who correctly perceived the threat to their autonomy and livelihood posed by medical men. Further, there was considerable ambivalence among patients and the general public about the propriety and legitimacy of male medical birth attendants, and even the corporate elite of the medical profession was vehemently opposed to medical intervention at births. Midwifery doctors had particular professional interests in hospital creation since the hospital setting afforded them special opportunities to legitimate their role and formally exercise power over midwives and patients, through immediately visible organisational means, but also more subtly by using hospital practice as a model which influenced wider social attitudes to birth in a manner favourable to doctors' interests. *Post facto* observation of midwifery doctors' activities show them to be the classic strategies of an occupational group engaging in a nascent process of professionalisation in the subordination of female competitors and the attempt to establish socially legitimate dominance over work activity and clientele. Theorists of the professions (Johnson, 1972; Freidson, 1974) have tended to ignore the fact that groups which have successfully achieved these ends have usually been male in composition. Midwifery doctors are but one example, and it seems clear that the ability to command the resources necessary for hospital foundation derived from wider social powers which their female rivals did not possess.

Midwifery and the medical profession

It is not generally realised that until the seventeenth century, midwifery in England had been a strictly non-medical lay craft which was quite marginal to the existing framework of medical practice, medical training, and medical corporate control. Although medical practice in this period was not very developed, medicine was formally and fairly rigidly organised into three well-defined estates of physician, barber-surgeon, and apothecary, each with related modes of training, apprenticeship and some form of corporate organisation.[5] Midwifery had no place in the training of any of these groups, it formed no part of the curriculum of either the university educated physician, or the apprenticeship of the barber-surgeon or apothecary. No medical licences were granted in midwifery and the care of women in labour was in no sense a medical responsibility, although pregnancy was occasionally mentioned in medical texts. All the sources on pre-seventeenth-century English midwifery confirm that it was a folk-craft, and, whilst it is possible that medical men did occasionally attend births, this would have been exceptional (Aveling, 1872; Radcliffe, 1967).

The formal exclusion of midwifery from medical practice was primarily due to the fact that from time immemorial it had been 'women's work'. The rise of the clerical universities from the thirteenth century and of the medical corporations from the sixteenth century onwards progressively excluded women from formal medical practice, so that by the seventeenth century the title 'medical' was gradually becoming identified with the male sex. The old Anglo-Saxon word 'midwife', meaning together or with ('mid'), and women ('wife'), neatly expressed the sex of the practitioner and the essentially informal communal nature of traditional childbirth management. In pre-industrial England, as in most pre-industrial societies, midwifery was seen as an extension of the female sex role, and was largely practised within the confines of a female subculture with only minimal male interference (Clark, 1919, pp. 265, 268; Culpeper, 1651; Maubray, 1724). Childbirth itself was but one of a series of natural life events through which most women passed, and an occasion for an often lively and somewhat alcoholic gathering of female neighbours and kin. It was customary to serve 'caudle', a thin gruel mixed with wine or ale, to the mother and her female attendants, thereby emphasising the social nature of the occasion for the female community (Ward, 1710). Mothers of all social strata, including royalty and the aristocracy, were delivered at home and records of female midwifery attendants to the English royal family date back to the fifteenth century (Aveling, 1872). All the evidence points to the existence of a taboo on direct male participation at childbirth either by kinfolk or physicians.

Female midwifery was, however, not an entirely informal or unofficial occupation. Between the sixteenth and early-eighteenth centuries, respectable matrons were granted ecclesiastical licences to practise the craft amongst the nobility and gentry.[6] By comparison with the self-governing medical corporations, ecclesiastical registration of midwifery would seem in theory to have been a highly repressive form of occupational control. However, in practical childbirth management 'professed' midwives enjoyed a considerable degree of occupational and clinical autonomy. The sixteenth-century church ruling that midwives should perform Caesarian section if necessary and remove and baptise the child, meant that the presence of either medical men or clerics in the birth chamber was rendered unnecessary, even where a physician was in residence in an aristocratic household.

In the course of the seventeenth century, former female pre-eminence in the occupation of midwifery was finally challenged. For reasons hitherto unexplained, we can discern a series of indicators of male medical incursion into the occupation: the appointment of the first male *accoucheur* to the English royal family; the increased translation of continental midwifery texts into English (since European midwifery was more highly developed in this period); and the publication in 1653 of the first medical text dealing with labour, by a native born Englishman, the celebrated physician William Harvey.[7]

By the end of the seventeenth century, the male medical midwifery practitioner was very much in evidence, and the inelegant and intrinsically contradictory title 'man-midwife' had entered the English language. Whilst it has been argued that not all men-midwives were recruited from the existent medical occupations, the evidence suggests that male midwifery was an overwhelmingly medical initiative, hence the terms 'man-midwife' and 'medical midwife' are used interchangeably hereafter in this chapter. In the course of the twentieth century, childbirth has frequently been treated and regarded as a surgical operation, although the natural childbirth movement has presented a strong challenge to this. Consequently, it is usually supposed that the earliest men-midwives were recruited primarily from the barber-surgeons' ranks. However this supposition is incorrect: men-midwives were self-recruited from the ranks of physicians, barber-surgeons and apothecaries, and many of the earliest recorded male midwives of the seventeenth century were physicians, e.g. the Chamberlens, Percival Willughby, and William Sermon to name but a few who appear in the roll of the Royal College of Physicians. Following continental fashion male midwifery seems to have been initially practised amongst the aristocracy, who often retained a physician as a member of the household, as much for his classical learning and polite conversation as for his medical skill (Jewson, 1974). The custom of calling for medical consultation at a childbirth seems to have progressively filtered down to the 'middling classes' who were much in evidence by the end of the century.

By the closing decades of the seventeenth century, the male midwives' attempts to bring midwifery under some sort of informal medical control were becoming manifest. The taboo on direct male attendance at childbirth still obtained fairly widely. Aristocratic mothers were still delivered predominantly by women, but increasingly a physician man-midwife was to be found in the background assuming a supervisory and consultative role. On 10 June 1687, for instance, Mrs Labany delivered the wife of James II of a son, receiving the enormous fee of 500 guineas, although Dr Hugh Chamberlen was officially supervising the case but was called away (Aveling, 1872, p. 114).

Medical men legitimated their presence by suggesting that they should intervene if complications arose. Very few medical men had actually performed or even seen deliveries, but this evidently did not deter them from attempting to teach midwives their craft, as the somewhat acid comments from a midwife of the period indicate (Cellier, 1687; original emphasis):

> I hope doctor these considerations will deter any of you from pretending to teach us Midwifery, especially such as confess *they never delivered Women in their lives*, and being asked *What they would do in such a case?* reply *they have not yet studied it*, but will when the occasion serves. But I doubt it will not satisfy the Women of this age, who are so sensible and impatient of their Pain, that few of them will be prevailed with to bear it in Complement to the Doctor, *while he fetches his Book*, studies the case and teaches the Midwife *to perform her work*, which she hopes may be done before he comes.

The emergence of a substantial mercantile middle class in the early-eighteenth century created an expanded market for medical services of all kinds, and large numbers of medical men attracted by the lucrative nature of the midwifery market began to take up the craft. In 1748 a royal physician and man-midwife attributed the growth of men-midwives 'to the necessity they are under of getting their bread in the best manner they can', and argued that there were now 'more Men-Midwives than streets in London' (Douglas, 1748). Whilst Douglas undoubtedly exaggerates, his comments are consistent with other impressionistic contemporary evidence on the growth of medical midwifery. In 1754 Benjamin Pugh, a man-midwife complained that 'every young surgeon now intends practising midwifery' (Pugh, 1754), whilst the classic biography of the well-known man-midwife, Dr Smellie, stresses the rapid growth of male midwifery practitioners in London in the period up to and around the mid-eighteenth century (Glaister, 1894).

Evidence from eighteenth-century sources about the extent to which medical men were engaged in, or wanted to engage in routine midwifery, as against the management of complicated or abnormal births, is not clear. The respective class and status of both doctors and patients appear to have been crucial variables. At one end of the continuum the rough Scottish apothecary William Smellie performed thousands of routine working-class deliveries, paying his patients a small sum for the privilege of delivering them in the presence of his male apprentices, whose tuition fees constituted his main source of income (Glaister, 1894). Amongst the 'middling classes' male as well as female practitioners appear to have performed routine deliveries. But it was the physicians with upper-class practices who particularly wanted to actively manage normal labours rather than merely wait in the wings as consultants. Philip Thicknesse (1764) commented on this practice:

> Who ushered two royal children into the world within these two years? Mrs. Draper. Do you think the life of both parties was not an object of the highest concern? Methinks I hear it said, but two doctors were in waiting in case any superior assistance should be wanted.

Hence it seems that persons of rank preferred to keep attending physicians in the background which put such doctors in rather a dilemma. For how could physicians be expected to intervene effectively in difficult labours if they had little idea except in theory as to how normal labours should progress? It evidently became a matter of some urgency for medical men to get experience of normal deliveries if they were to retain any credibility.

Although doctors' previous attempts to supervise female midwives' work had already begun to erode the occupational status of female practitioners, attempts by many medical men to engage in routine midwifery constituted a direct attack on the female midwife's livelihood, and brought fierce competition between the sexes in the midwifery market. In most rural areas midwifery practice probably continued according to the traditional female-dominated model; however, in urban areas such as London, in the 1740s and 1750s, midwifery had become a crowded and highly competitive occupation. A flood of polemical literature from mid-century testifies to the acrimony of the dispute between male and female practitioners. Protagonists of both sexes did their best to discredit each other; a male surgeon (Aveling, 1872, pp. 125-6) claimed that:

> Midwives cram their patients with cordials, keeping them intoxicated during the time they are in labour,

> driving poor women up and down stairs, notwithstanding their shrieks and shaking them so violently as to bring on convulsion fits on pretence of hastening their labours.

The formidable Mrs Nihell (Nihell, 1760) who had completed a midwifery apprenticeship at the prestigious Hotel Dieu in Paris, felt:

> An insuppressible indignation at the errors and pernicious innovations introduced into (midwifery) and every day gaining ground . . . sillily fostering a preference of men to women in the practice of midwifery . . . (by) that multitude of disciples of Dr. Smellie . . . those self-constituted men-midwives made out of broken barbers, tailors or even pork butchers, for I know myself one of this last trade, who after passing half his life in stuffing sausages, is turned an intrepid physician and man-midwife. See the whole pack open in full cry: to arms, to arms is the word: and what are those arms by which they maintain themselves, but those instruments, those weapons of death.

Apart from threatened female practitioners, a certain amount of concerted opposition to male medical midwifery was building up in a number of other quarters. Paradoxically, perhaps the most important source of opposition came from within the ranks of the medical profession itself. The elite governing bodies of the medical corporations of physicians and surgeons, which were the principal *loci* of professional power and legitimation, did not regard midwifery as a proper or respectable medical endeavour. As far as the Fellows of the medical corporations were concerned, midwifery was a demeaning manual operation best left to 'old women'; if medical men continued to do 'old women's' work then the status and prestige of the medical professional as a whole might be lowered. The Fellows of the Royal College of Physicians expressed their disapproval of midwifery by refusing to admit more than ten men-midwives to the Fellowship in the course of the eighteenth century (Munk, 1861).

After 1748 the Surgeons' Company banned men-midwives from its Court of Assistants (Hamilton, 1951); men-midwives therefore found themselves excluded from the main arenas of corporate medical professional power.

Reaction to medical midwifery, and a similarly intransigent attitude to its practitioners, was also very much in evidence in the voluntary hospital system. With the exception of the Middlesex, physicians and surgeons in the acute general hospitals refused to admit maternity patients, placing them together with small children, 'persons disordered in their senses', and those suffering from 'Venereal Disease', 'the Pox', and the dying and incurable, as people who were categorically excluded. This policy was maintained by most general hospitals until well into the nineteenth century (Woodward, 1974; Abel-Smith, 1964). Both Woodward and Abel-Smith have suggested that maternity cases were excluded from general hospitals because of hospital consultants' fears about perceived risks to other patients from puerpural sepsis. In the light of the extremely primitive knowledge in this era about the aetiology and transmission of infection, this is unlikely; it is more probable that the exclusion of maternity cases from general hospitals was motivated primarily by the prestigious hospital consultants' derisory attitudes to midwifery and their refusal to associate themselves with a practice of which they disapproved. This attitude, coupled with the medical corporations' refusal to grant any formal professional status to this new medical role, retarded a more widespread social acceptance of the practice.

By challenging the traditional norm of female attendance at childbirth, male midwives had to contend with two other main forms of hostility. The first was based on sexual prudery. The gross indecency, violation of female modesty, and the very threat to married life supposedly occasioned by male access to the female body during labour and delivery, were frequently raised by critics of male midwives. The second was the insistence that childbirth was after all a natural event, not a medical emergency. The care of women in labour, it was argued, was best left to 'that excellent and never failing midwife, "Goody Nature" and medical men had no business meddling in childbirth at all' (Thicknesse, 1764).

By the mid-eighteenth century a paradoxical and contradictory situation obtained. Evidently men-midwives had achieved some degree of social acceptance with their patients, otherwise the practice could not have developed so quickly or extensively. Nevertheless, competition from female practitioners, opposition from the principal professional power groups, and a fairly widespread belief in certain sections of society that the care of women in labour was neither an appropriate nor a legitimate medical endeavour, constituted serious handicaps to medical midwives' ambitions. If medical midwives were to develop their group interests, gain vital clinical experience and ultimately legitimate the new occupational role they were trying to create for themselves, they had to find some means of overcoming at least some of these handicaps, and hospital provision for maternity cases might provide some solutions.

Professional imperatives and the hospital

First, if competition from female practitioners was to be diffused, the man-midwife had to find some means of formally and unambiguously defining himself as the preferred and apparently superior midwifery attendant. In practice this was extremely problematic for two reasons. First, the clinical skills of the two groups of practitioners were barely distinguishable; the female midwife was often more experienced than the doctor, and patients often preferred women. There was one technological difference between the two groups, which historians of midwifery have regarded as extremely important: namely, the medical invention of the obstetric forceps which became public in 1733.[8] Medical historians have argued that the forceps gave medical men an immediate advantage over midwives, and that the forceps was the single most important factor in the medical conquest of midwifery (Aveling, 1872, p. 118; Radcliffe, 1947, p. 56). Since historians of midwifery have generally been obstetricians, it is hardly surprising that they would stress the technical progress represented by the forceps. However, it is hardly likely that a single isolated technical advance could have accounted for the medical conquest of midwifery.

Whilst the forceps was invaluable for obstructed deliveries, even in the eighteenth century, these occurred more rarely than is usually supposed, as the more successful midwifery doctors of the period made clear. One claimed that 'there is little occasion for the present *frequent use of instruments*, that excepting in a *Case* or *two* which but *rarely* happen' (Manningham, 1744; original emphasis). Even Dr Smellie, who was primarily responsible for popularising the forceps, argued that it was only necessary in 10 out of 10,000 cases (Smellie, 1752). Another doctor reporting on a series of 1,897 deliveries between 1774 and 1781, claimed that in 80 'unnatural' or 'laborious' labours the forceps had to be used only four times! (Bland, 1781). In addition, as many commentators make clear, patients were very frightened of instruments 'which carry so much horror along with them for . . . *Mother* or *Child* (who) too often suffer greatly by the Use of *Instruments*' (Manningham, 1744; original emphasis). Further, in the pre-antiseptic era instrumental interference would have inevitably transmitted an infection, usually fatal. Hence, although the obstetric forceps would have given medical men the advantage in a few complicated or 'laborious' deliveries, in general the abuse of midwifery instruments including the forceps by less skilled doctors, discredited medical midwives as a whole, exposed them to criticism and hostility from many quarters, and is one of the main themes of the opponents of medical midwifery (Nihell, 1760; Thicknesse, 1764).

Second, if the medical man was to present himself as the midwifery practitioner of preference, he required some degree of power over client preferences. Even the London slum patients of Dr Smellie were paid for their co-operation with him and were usually delivered under a sheet. Most medical midwives practised among patients of an equal or superior class position to themselves who were even more accustomed to defining the mode of doctor-patient interaction; consequently, client-control generally predominated over doctor-control in upper-class medical practice (Jewson, 1974). Within a context of client-control, the medical midwife whose own social and professional status was decidedly anomalous, was in no position to press his claims and demands on the upper-class client, and thereby define the character of client preferences in his own favour. The man-midwife therefore had difficulty in overcoming resistance based on sexual prudery, which denied him access to the intimacy of the patient's body, and prevented the man-midwife's acquisition of vital clinical experience and expertise. Status differentials between doctors and patients of a higher social class created a social distance between them expressed via minimal body contact. In wanting to employ the techniques of vaginal examination and per vagina manipulation of the foetus used by women, male midwifery practitioners were challenging ancient sexual *mores* of access to the female body during birth. They were also, in their capacity as doctors, violating the norm of minimal body contact in eighteenth-century patient-doctor interaction which relied primarily on subjective reporting by patients and on symptoms rather than on clinical examination by the doctor.

Finally, if midwifery was to be successfully incorporated into medicine, the medical midwife had to confront the belief embodied in the traditional lay mode of childbirth management, that birth was a normal natural physiological event. In order to challenge this belief, medical men had to be able to stress those aspects of parturition which were potentially complicated and dangerous, and which would therefore seem to legitimately require the attention of a doctor. The type of institution most suited to the medical midwife's various professionalising requirements, namely the restriction of competition from female practitioners, the establishment of doctor-control over client preferences, the acquisition of clinical experience, and the depiction of childbirth as potentially hazardous, was some sort of hospital provision for maternity patients. The structure and characteristics of the eighteenth-century charitable hospital could meet these requirements in a number of ways.

The hospital was characterised by a high degree of formal doctor-control which permitted the definition and enforcement of an occupational hierarchy, in which the relative roles, responsibilities and status of doctors and midwives could be unambiguously delineated. Secondly, since hospitals were charitable enterprises, they only received patients of low social class and status. Such patients would constitute a relatively passive clientele, which would be powerless in the face of, and unable to challenge, medical aims and demands, including those related to body access. Hospital patients would thereby provide an ample source of clinical material. If the clinical facilities offered by the hospital increased the man-midwife's knowledge and expertise as a medical practitioner, he might hope for greater recognition from his colleagues in other spheres of the medical profession. Further, the practice of midwifery in a distinctively medical setting such as a hospital, could be expected to convey to the public at large the notion that childbirth management was a legitimately medical, rather than a lay or family concern. Hospital consultancies had additional advantages. They carried intangible status assets, conferred prestige on practitioners, enhanced professional reputations in the broadest sense, and could therefore be expected to attract wealthy patients to the consultants' private practice.

The professional advantages which a maternity hospital could offer midwifery practitioners had been raised a number of times from the late-seventeenth century. One of the earliest and most radical proposals had come from the female midwife, Elizabeth Cellier, who in 1687 sent a plan to James II for a network of twelve parochial lying-in hospitals in London to be administered by an autonomous 'corporation of skilful female midwives' (Cellier, 1687). Although James II appears to have regarded the principle of the plan favourably, Mrs Cellier's past reputation as a Papist and political radical did not enhance her cause, and, as was customary in those days, the plan was referred to the Royal College of Physicians. Members of the College were by that time engaged in midwifery, and were therefore in direct competition with midwives. Although the Fellows disapproved of their members' midwifery practice, it was nevertheless incumbent upon them to protect the interests of College licentiates. Consequently the physicians' corporation vehemently opposed a plan which would probably enhance the occupational status of female practitioners, and would additionally give them autonomous secular powers, and formal training facilities.

For somewhat different reasons, probably lack of financial support, the later-seventeenth-century proposal of the man-midwife, Hugh Chamberlen, also failed to come to fruition. Early-eighteenth-century proposals of other men-midwives also came to nothing (Maubray 1724, Douglas 1736).[9] The men-midwives' plans evidently posited medical, rather than midwife control of the maternity hospital. Whichever group might control a maternity institution, it was not until 1739 that the first medically directed maternal hospital provision in England was created in an infirmary in Westminster. As the founder of this enterprise commented (Manningham, 1739):

> It has often indeed been a Matter of Surprise to me, as well as to many others, that in this our great opulent City, an Hospital for taking care of poor Women labouring of Child has been thus long neglected. . . . Tho' I freely confess, I am not without Great Hopes of one Day seeing proper Measures taken by the legislature of establishing an Hospital of this kind.

The eighteenth-century state was not prepared to intervene in the provision of acute general hospitals, let alone maternity hospitals, and eighteenth-century hospitals were entirely financed by private capital.

Philanthropy, infantile mortality, and the foundation of the 'lying-in' hospitals

Although limited medical relief was available under the old Poor Law, provision for childbearing women was sparse and uneven. By the middle decades of the eighteenth century, the plans of the medical midwives for the creation of maternity hospitals were able to attract considerable funds from philanthropists. The willingness of philanthropists to invest their private capital in maternity hospitals was closely related to fears about depopulation, and widespread concern about the extremely high infant-mortality rate.

Although historians of the eighteenth century locate the depopulation debate much later in the century, there was considerable concern from 1739 onwards that population was falling. In London the catastrophic levels of mortality in general, and among infants and children in particular, were clearly shown by the Parish Registers and London Bills of Mortality; in the first half of the eighteenth century burials exceeded baptisms by three to two, and, according to the available records, births in London did not exceed deaths until 1788. From 1728 onwards age at death was recorded in the Bills of Mortality, which revealed that 74 per cent of the total London death rate was accounted for by children under five years of age (George, 1925, appendices B and C, p. 406). Although Hanway did not publish all his results until the 1760s, the high levels of infant mortality had already been widely publicised by Coram, and the governors of the Foundling Hospital.

This terrible wastage of life in London coincided with periodic shortages of labour, and the country was almost continuously at war from 1739. An ever expanding demand for labourers and servicemen meant that the apparent depopulation of the capital in particular and probably of the country in general had become a serious issue. The census of 1811 would in fact reveal that fears about depopulation had been erroneous. Nevertheless, for the eighteenth-century adherents of the depopulation theory, any proposals which could have some impact on the perceived problem were likely to be given consideration.

The appalling social conditions in which the mass of the London population lived, infectious diseases, and a whole variety of other social variables were probably the principal cause of the high infant-death rate. However, medical men viewed the issue rather differently, and were of the opinion that the incompetence of female midwives was one of the main causes of infant and maternal death. This accusation had been made frequently by men-midwives since they had entered the field. Medical historians have generally overlooked the technical incompetence of male practitioners, so vehemently denounced by Nicholls (1751). In deploring the standards of male midwifery and the numbers of children they destroyed, Nicholls says:

> Of all the Practitioners who exercise the different Branches of Physick, the Man-Midwives alone (as such) give no Test of their Learning, Dexterity or Integrity; and yet these Men are permitted on their single Opinions avowedly and professedly to kill our children, and to treat our Wives in such a manner as frequently ends in their destruction.

Whilst Nicholls's style is polemical, his arguments are put forward by other contemporaries, and undoubtedly have some factual basis which the majority of medical historians have preferred to ignore. Whatever the truth of the matter, there was considerable public concern about general standards of midwifery practice. Within this climate of anxiety about depopulation, high infant mortality, and the state of midwifery practice, medical men were able to argue with some success for the establishment of maternity hospitals, supposedly to raise standards of midwifery practice, and thereby improve the chances of survival of at least some infants.

Consequently, considerable private funds were forthcoming, and six maternity foundations were created in London between 1739 and 1765. The foundation of the London lying-in institutions was entirely the result of the success of entrepreneurial medical intiative in attracting private capital. In their financial and administrative structure the lying-in hospitals were organised in the same manner as the acute general hospitals. Charitable subscribers to the hospitals undertook some of the ongoing administrative and fund-raising work, which gave them the right of recommending a certain number of patients annually to the hospital. Evidently only the better connected medical midwives could expect to attract financial support for their plans, and significantly of the six London lying-in institutions, five were the sole initiative of the more prestigious university educated physicians, and only one hospital was founded by a group of the lower status surgeons, i.e. The City Lying In, founded by Richard Ball, Surgeon, and William Ball, Surgeon-

Apothecary, with 'eight other gentlemen' (City Lying In minutes 1750-6, in R. Cannings, 1922).

In 1739 one of the most fashionable physician man-midwives in London, Richard Manningham, had succeeded in having a lying-in ward created at St James's Infirmary, Westminster. Very little is known about this institution apart from Manningham's own accounts of it, but it probably survived until at least 1744. The foundation of Manningham's lying-in ward was closely connected with the campaign to reduce infant mortality, since his ward evidently shared support with Coram's Foundling Hospital which had been created to care for abandoned infants. A joint advertisement extolling the merits of the two institutions had appeared in a London newspaper to solicit funds for the charities, and was reprinted by Richard Manningham (copy bound with Manningham, 1744).

Two years after the foundation of the Middlesex Hospital a lying-in ward was opened there in 1747. By 1749 the medical men in the Middlesex lying-in department were so pleased with the success of their venture that they proposed converting the entire Middlesex Hospital into a lying-in institution. This plan met with great resistance from doctors in other departments, and from the majority of the governors. Most of the medical men from the lying-in department resigned, and together with some of the governors, resolved to set up their own separate institution for the sole reception of maternity patients (Middlesex Hospital weekly board minutes, 1749, in Wilson, 1845, pp. 10-13). The result of their efforts was the first separate maternity hospital in London, the British Lying In which opened late in 1749 (*An Account of the Lying In Hospital, Brownlow St*, 1771). This was rapidly followed by other medical initiatives which resulted in the City Lying In in 1750, followed by the General Lying In in 1752 (which became Queen Charlotte's in 1809), and the New Westminster Lying In in 1765 (which was subsequently called the General Lying In in 1819). (*An account of the City of London Lying in Hospital*, 1767; *An account of the Rise . . . of the General Lying In*, 1768; *General Lying In*, 1830).

Medical power in the hospital setting

Like the acute general hospitals, the lying-in institutions accorded doctors a considerable degree of power over the definition of the internal structure of the hospital, and its mode of operation in terms of staffing arrangements and patient care. Medical midwives in most cases automatically became governors of the hospitals, sat on their main administrative bodies[10] and played a large part in formulating the rules and standing orders of the institutions pertaining to the matron, nurses, and patients, who all came under medical jurisdiction.[11] What was the position of female midwives *vis-à-vis* these institutions at the time of their foundation? All of the lying-in institutions initially excluded the employment of female midwives apart from the matron; although all of the institutions except the Middlesex ultimately instructed female pupils in the nineteenth century. The first two lying-in wards, i.e. Manningham's ward and the Middlesex ward, did not employ a matron at all, and deliveries were conducted solely by medical midwives and their male apprentices. Nor did these two institutions employ midwives to care for patients in the antenatal or post-natal period; the Middlesex ward employed one 'monthly nurse' for the ongoing care of patients (Wilson, 1845, pp. 7-8) who were usually admitted in the last month of pregnancy and remained in hospital for one month after delivery, the customary period of 'lying-in'.

In the four other institutions medical monopoly of deliveries was not complete, since a midwife-matron was employed, who was expected to attend all normal deliveries. However, within the hospital structure her clinical role in midwifery was played down in relation to her other role responsibilities. The matron-midwife was expected to act as a housekeeper; she was responsible for the day-to-day running of the hospital, for maintenance of 'the orderly conduct of patients and nurses', and for the supervision of diet, laundry and the sewing of 'childbed linen' by the patients. The matron was formally designated as subordinate to the medical faculty, she was to obey them in all matters, and stringent rules pertained to her personal conduct and character. She was forbidden to leave the hospital premises without permission, or to engage in private practice outside the hospital (weekly board minutes, General Lying In, 1776-1810). The medical men who were part-time consultants of course enjoyed considerable private practices. The matron-midwife was very clearly defined as a subordinate and inferior type of midwifery practitioner in the hospital structure.

It could be objected that the hospital definition of the midwife's subordinate position had very little impact on her position in private practice, or upon wider social perceptions of the midwife's and doctor's respective roles. But in fact knowledge of hospital hierarchies had fairly wide currency. Each hospital had a large number of subscribers who were quite conversant with its internal staffing arrangements. Lady subscribers were especially invited to visit the hospitals and observe the arrangements made for patients, and the conduct of staff. The subservient position of the matron-midwife *vis-à-vis* the medical men can hardly have escaped the notice of the lady visitors, who, when pregnant themselves, might well be expected to request the attendance of a medical midwife, rather than a traditional female practitioner. Further, the lying-in institutions published frequent pamphlets, setting out the rules of the institutions, and stating clearly the merits of their arrangements, particularly the importance of medical supervision of maternity patients. The medical definition of the midwife as an inferior and subordinate type of midwifery practitioner must therefore have become widely known, and did nothing to enhance the status of those midwives engaged in private practice.

One of the objects of founding lying-in institutions had been to afford extended possibilities for medical experience of routine deliveries. Although the rules and orders of the institutions stated that medical men in theory primarily attended complicated cases, in practice the hospital case-books, where they survive, show that medical men attended a considerable number of routine deliveries. Furthermore, medical men saw all the patients on admission and discharge ('Register of Patients, General Lying In, February, 1798-July 1807'). The large number of patients who passed annually through the hospitals provided doctors with an ample and varied source of clinical material.[12]

Female modesty, which in fashionable society had been such a handicap to the medical midwife, constituted no such problem in the hospital setting. It was evidently assumed that working-class women were neither modest nor retiring about their bodily functions, since all deliveries took place in open wards until approximately 1860, when the first separate labour wards were provided (Gunn, 1964, p. 96). Doctor-control over the working-class client was largely possible because of her subordinate class position, but the patient's passivity was further ensured by the social-control ethos of the charitable hospital. Patients had to obey both doctors and the matron, and stringent rules pertaining to personal conduct, religious observance, and the injunction to appear properly grateful for services rendered, together with the possibility of being discharged for what was termed 'any irregularity' and never admitted again, acted as powerful reinforcements of client compliance to medical demands.

Why were working-class women so willing to subject themselves to the indignities they so obviously endured in the lying-in hospital? The poor and exploited rarely leave any written documentation for the historian. We can therefore only examine the way in which the objective social conditions of the working-class mother's life might have impelled her to give birth in hospital. The medical and non-medical sources of the period show that the living conditions and poverty of many working-class women in London must have been so extreme as to have permitted few viable choices about the setting in which they might give birth, and it was not uncommon for women to be confined in doorways, churchyards or in the street. Extensive migration into London and the rapid spread of urbanisation over surrounding areas had led to overcrowding and appalling housing conditions (George, 1925), and had probably broken down many traditional female kin networks within which lower-class parturient women had traditionally received care.

Further, poverty was often extreme, and from mid-century less than subsistence level wages meant that even the small fee of one and sixpence charged by a charity midwife for a domiciliary delivery (Royal Maternity Charity minutes, 1765) would have been beyond the reach of many working-class women. It is indicative of the poverty common in this period that many of the outdoor maternity charities had to lend their patients 'childbed linen' for the period of confinement which were then washed and reused for other patients. Although written to solicit funds from the charitable, the lying-in hospitals' own publications are an eloquent testament to the deprivations suffered by poor women. The first publication by Queen Charlotte's Hospital claims that the institution's main goal was 'to rescue from the deepest despair, and the horrors of perishing with their unoffending Babies, in the open streets and fields . . . unhappy objects of female despair and distress' (*An Account of the Rise, Progress and State of the General Lying In* (Queen Charlotte's, 1768)). Queen Charlotte's was unusual in so far as it accepted those in greatest need, i.e. unmarried mothers and extra-parochial immigrants who between 1755 and 1765 constituted its largest single groups of patients (New Laws, Rules and Orders, 1809). Nevertheless the poverty and distress of lying-in hospital patients is mentioned frequently in the publications of other hospitals, and is perhaps best summed up by the following remarks from a fund-raising sermon preached on behalf of the City Lying In in 1767 (Nichols, 1767; original emphasis):

> It [childbirth] is a distress of such extremity . . . *that the children were come to the birth, and there was not strength to bring forth*. This is often the deplorable condition of those applying for this Charity; *they have no strength*, no means, no necessaries of their own provided, no proper help or attendance for sustaining the ordinary, much less the unusual pains and perils of that season; none at all, but what they happily find in this House of Mercy.

If the working-class mother's body and human dignity were of little or no consequence in the hospital setting, at least the hospital guaranteed her material subsistence during and after confinement, even if she was in severe want for the rest of her childbearing cycle. This in itself must have been a powerful incentive to seek hospital admission whatever other humiliation had to be endured.

The ideological medicalisation of childbirth via the milieu of the hospital becomes increasingly obvious in the printed publications of the lying-in institutions. The hazardous and potentially dangerous facets of parturition receive the greatest emphasis, the importance of medical intervention in the case of complications which supposedly arose in almost any birth were stressed, and the 'timely assistance' of medical men ever ready to save mothers from the disastrous consequences of birth were frequently pointed out. As far as the lying-in hospital literature was concerned, parturition had become a medical emergency, rather than a normal everyday event. Although medical therapy had little to offer if fatal complications occurred, the management of complicated as well as routine midwifery cases was increasingly accepted as a legitimate medical concern by large sections of fashionable society.

Postscript

It is not easy to assess the effects of lying-in hospitals in procuring the gradual medical conquest of midwifery, since controversies continued to surround men-midwives' activities and are dealt with in detail elsewhere.[13] Throughout the nineteenth century debates continued as to the appropriateness of male medical management of birth, the use of instruments, home versus hospital delivery, and the status of female practitioners. Nevertheless it seems clear that lying-in hospitals brought immediate professional rewards to doctors, clinical experience gained in hospital was invaluable in men-midwives' private work, and the lying-in hospital consultants rapidly became an obstetric elite. The lying in hospital designation of the midwife as subordinate to the doctor provided a model which was widely reproduced elsewhere. Evidently many midwives tried to continue in independent unsupervised private practice, but by the beginning of the nineteenth century had to compete with rapidly growing numbers of general practitioners who regarded midwifery as fundamental to their task and income. In specialist as well as in general private practice, midwives if employed at all, were progressively seen as little more than nursing assistants to 'watch at labours' and care for the mother during the month of lying-in, i.e. as a 'monthly nurse'. Donnison claims that in the 1841 Census only a tiny number of women were described as midwives, although many 'handywomen' probably continued to do deliveries in rural areas. The corporate elite of the medical profession maintained its opposition to man-midwifery for some time and throughout the nineteenth century many mothers wanted their labours supervised by women, whilst groups of female midwives and their supporters fought for the reinstatement of the female practitioner. Some wanted a single equal midwifery qualification for men and women, whilst others joined in attempts to secure female entry to medical practice itself (Donnison, 1977). But the men-midwives were not easily defeated and demanded superordinate status and recognition as self-styled experts on childbirth which they finally achieved with the second Medical Registration Act of 1886 which introduced midwifery into the basic medical curriculum. By contrast, female midwives found their subordinate status confirmed by the 1902 Midwife Act which put a majority of medical men on the council responsible for the training and registration of midwives, thereby making clear that neither skilled women nor mothers could regard birth as their own concern any more.

Notes

1 This chapter is dedicated to my son Philippe. Comments on an earlier version of this chapter were given by Margot Jefferys, Margaret Stacey, Celia Davies and Hilary Graham. Source material was made available by the librarian of the Royal College of Obstetricians and Gynaecologists; the Wellcome Institute Library for the History of Medicine; the Secretary to Queen Charlotte's Hospital; the archivist of the Middlesex Hospital, J.L. Thornton; the librarian to St Bartholomew's Hospital; and the staff of the Public Records Office.

2 In 1739 and 1747 respectively maternity wards were created in St James's Infirmary, Westminster, and the Middlesex Hospital. Subsequently four separate maternity hospitals appeared in London; they were: British Lying In (1749); City of London Lying In (1950); General Lying In (1752, which became Queen Charlotte's); New Westminster Lying In (1765, which became the General Lying In). Apart from the Rotunda Hospital, Dublin, created in 1745, the provincial hospitals were: Newcastle-upon-Tyne Lying-In Charity (1760, later Princess Mary Maternity Hospital); Manchester Lying In Charity (1790, later St Mary's Hospital); Edinburgh Lying In Hospital (1793, later Simpson Memorial Maternity Pavilion); Humane Female Society for the Relief of Lying-in Women (1794, later Royal Maternity Hospital, Belfast); Cork Lying In Hospital (1798).

3 The following figures were computed from hospital records:

1750-67, City Lying In: average number of deliveries per annum 349

1749-70, British Lying In: average number of deliveries per annum 479

1755-65, Queen Charlotte's: average number of deliveries per annum 876

In London in 1770 the total number of recorded baptisms in the parish registers was 19,789 (M.D. George, 1925, Appendix 1, p. 404).

4 The first was the Royal Maternity Charity, London, founded in 1757; another fifteen outdoor lying-in charities in London were added between 1774 and 1789 (Highmore, 1814). These continued to proliferate in London and the provinces in the nineteenth century (unpublished sources, Wellcome Institute Library for the History of Medicine, London; and Public Records Office).

5 The Royal College of Physicians was formed in 1518, the Barber Surgeons' Company in 1540; the apothecaries were united in a guild company with grocers and druggists until 1617, when they became the Society of Apothecaries. On modes of training, clinical responsibilities, and boundaries between the three medical occupations, see histories of the respective medical corporations. For an overview, see V.L. Bullough, 1966; N. Parry, and J. Parry, 1976, ch. 6; B. Hamilton, 1951.

6 On ecclesiastical licensing of midwives see Chapter I in Aveling. For a twenty-years' period between 1642 and 1662, female midwives were licensed by the Barber Surgeons' Company. On this point see E. Cellier, *To Dr – An Answer to his Queries concerning the Colledge of Midwives*.

7 The exact date of the appointment of the first Royal Accoucheur is not clear, but it was Peter Chamberlen who was appointed between 1614 and 1628. On the translation of continental midwifery texts into English see pp. 80-99, in H. Graham, 1960.

William Harvey first published *De Generatione Animalium* – including the chapter 'De Partu', dealing with labour – in 1651; this work became available in English in 1653.

8 The obstetric forceps had been invented by Peter Chamberlen in the seventeenth century and remained a family secret until its pattern was published by Edmund Chapman. Chapman's work went through at least three editions and one reprint in the period up to 1759. The forceps was refined by Smellie, Palfryn, and Giffard.

9 In 1716 John Bellers, together with a group of medical men, had founded the Westminster Society to 'provide a comprehensive service for sick and pregnant women' (Woodward, 1974, p. 11). The enterprise did not survive for more than several months because of lack of funds. As to whether it was an in-patient or out-patient institution is not clear, but it was probably an out-patient dispensary.

10 In the case of the Middlesex lying-in ward, medical midwives who were employed there after the attempt to turn the whole hospital into a maternity institution, had their executive powers curtailed by the lay governors; in the other hospitals, however, medical men automatically became governors. In the early years of both the General Lying In and Queen Charlotte's, medical power was abused. Dr Leake, founder of the General Lying In, kept the entire financial and administrative management of the hospital in his own hands for the first twenty years of its existence (*Notes from the Records of the General Lying in Hospital*, 1884, p. 3). Sometime after its foundation, Queen Charlotte's became the private property of two doctors who accommodated themselves in the lying-in ward, banished the patients and nurses to the attic, and lived in considerable style on the hospital funds (recorded in Chapter I of T. Ryan, 1886, see under Hospital Records, Queen Charlotte's Hospital).

11 See lying-in hospital publications.

12 See n. 3, op. cit.

13 M. Versluysen, 'Man-Midwife to Obstetrician: A Study in Occupational and Social Change, 1640-1886.' Ph.D. thesis (in progress), University of London.

Material relating to lying-in hospitals and charities

Unpublished sources

Public Records Office, London: 'An Introduction to the Records of the General Lying in Hospital, Westminster'. Records from the General Lying In Hospital, Westminster: 'Weekly Board Minutes 1776-1852'; 'Register of Patients, Feb 1798-July 1807'; 'Medical Officer's Case

Book 1827'; 'Admissions Registers, 1767-1798'; 'Register of Deliveries, Feb 1798-July 1807'.

Queen Charlotte's Hospital, London: 'Landmarks in the History of Queen Charlotte's Hospital'; 'Record of Examintion of Patients as to Marital Status, 1816'; 'Rules, Orders and Regulations for the Government of Queen Charlotte's Lying in Hospital, 1823'.

Royal College of Obstetricians and Gynaecologists, London: 'Royal Maternity Charity, Minutes 1761-1800'.

Printed works

An Account of the British Lying-in Hospital for Married Women, in Brownlow St, Long Acre, from its institution in November 1749, to December 1st 1770, c. 1771, London.

An account of the City of London Lying in Hospital for Married Women, in Ladersgate St., Instituted March 30, 1750, 1767, London.

An account of the General Lying in Hospital (Westminster), 1835, London.

An account of the rise and progress of the Lying in Hospital for Married Women . . . in Brownlow St. London, 1808, London.

An account of the Rise, Progress and State of the General Lying in Hospital, the corner of Quebec St, Oxford Rd (Queen Charlotte's), 1768, London.

An Act for the better Regulation of Lying in Hospitals, and other Places, appropriated for the Charitable reception of pregnant Women; and also to provide for the Settlement of Bastard Children, born in such Hospitals and Places, Geo. III, 1773, London.

Bi-Centenary Celebration 1765-1965 (General Lying In Hospital Westminster), 1965, London.

City of London Lying In Hospital, 'Weekly Board Minutes', cited in R.B. Cannings, *The City of London Maternity Hospital*, 1922, London.

General Lying in Hospital London Instituted 1765 incorporated 1830 (Westminster), 1830, London.

Highmore, A., *Pietas Londinensis: The History and Design and Present State of the Various Public Charities in and Near London*, 1814, London.

'Laws of the Middlesex Hospital Lying in Department, 1747' and 'Weekly Board Minutes of Middlesex Hospital Lying in Ward, 1748-9', cited in E. Wilson, *The History of the Middlesex Hospital During the First Century of its Existence, Compiled from the Hospital Records*, 1845, London.

Laws, Orders and Regulations and a list of Governors and Subscribers of Queen Charlotte's Hospital, London, 1828, London.

Manningham, R., *The Institution and Oeconomy of the Charitable*

Infirmary for the Relief of Poor Women in Labour..., 1739, London.

Manningham, R., *The Copy of the Paper published in the Daily Advertiser, by a Benefactor to the Foundling Hospital, setting forth the Benefit and Usefulness of this Charitable Undertaking*, c. 1740. Bound with *The Preface to Sir Richard Manningham's Latin Compendium of Midwifery, Women's and Children's Diseases English'd*, 1744, London.

Manningham, R., *An Abstract of Midwifery for the Use of the Lying in Infirmary*, 1744, London.

Manningham, R., *An Account of St. James' parochial lying in Infirmary at Westminster London*, 1744, London.

New Laws, Rules and Orders of the Queen's Lying in Hospital at Bayswater. . . . Instituted in January 1752 (Queen Charlotte's), 1809, London.

Nichols, John, *A sermon preached at the Parish Church of St Andrew, Holborn on Thurs. March 26, 1767 before (officers) of the City of London Lying in Hospital for married women*, 1767, London.

Plan of the Queen's Lying in Hospital. . . . London (Queen Charlotte's), 1817, London.

Ryan, T., *The History of Queen Charlotte's Lying in Hospital from its foundation in 1752 to the present time. With an Account of its Objects and Present State*, 1886, London.

References

Abel-Smith, B., *The Hospitals*, Heinemann, London, 1964.

Aveling, J.H. *English Midwives*, D.R. Hillman & Sons, Frome, 1872.

Berkeley, Sir G.H.A.C., 'The Teaching of Midwifery based on the Lloyds Roberts Memorial Lecture', *Journal of Obstetrics and Gynaecology of the British Empire*, vol. 37, no. 4, Winter 1929.

Bland, R., *Some Calculations . . . from the Midwifery Reports of the Westminster General Dispensary*, London, 1781.

Bullough, V.L., 'The Emergence of Medicine as a Profession', *Twentieth International Congress of History of Medicine, Proceedings*, 1966, pp. 605-10.

Cape, A., *The Royal College of Surgeons of England*, Royal College of Surgeons of England, London, 1959.

Cellier, E., 'A scheme for the foundation of a Royal Hospital . . . by and for the maintenance of a corporation of skilful midwives', June 1687, Folio manuscript of papers addressed to James II. Reprinted in Aveling, J.H., pp. 76-82.

Cellier, E., *To Dr – An Answer to his Queries Concerning the Colledge of Midwives*, London, 1687.

Chapman, E., *A treatise on the improvement of midwifery chiefly with regard to the operation*, 2nd edn, Brindley, London, 1735.

Clark, A., *The Working Life of Women in the Seventeenth Century*, George Routledge & Sons, London, 1919.

Culpeper, N., *The Directory for Midwives*, London, 1651.

Donnison, J., *Midwives and Medical Men*, Heinemann, London, 1977.

Douglas, J., *A short account of the state of midwifery in London*, Westminster, London, 1736.

Douglas, W., *A Letter to Dr. Smellie*, printed for J. Roberts, London, 1748.

Freidson, E., *Profession of Medicine*, Dodd Mead, New York, 1974.

George, M.D., *London Life in the Eighteenth Century*, Kegan Paul, London, 1925.

Gilliatt, W., 'Maternal Mortality. Stillbirth and NeoNatal Mortality', in J.M. Kerr (ed.), 1954.

Glaister, J., *Dr. W. Smellie and his Contemporaries*, James Nackhose, Glasgow, 1894.

Graham, H., *Eternal Eve – The Mysteries of Birth and the Customs that Surround it*, Hutchinson, London, 1960.

Granville, A.B., *A report on the practice of midwifery at the Westminster General Dispensary during 1818*, Burgess & Hill, London, 1819.

Gunn, A., 'Maternity Hospitals', in Poynter F.N.L. (ed.), *The Evolution of Hospitals in Britain*, Pitman Medical Publishing, London, 1964.

Hamilton, B., 'The Medical Profession in the Eighteenth Century', *Economic History Review*, vol, IV, no. 2, 1951.

Holland, E., 'The Medical Schools and the Teaching of Midwifery', in J.M. Kerr (ed.), 1954.

Illingworth, C., *The Story of William Hunter*, E. & S. Livingstone, Edinburgh, 1967.

Jewson, N.D., 'Medical Knowledge and the Patronage System in Eighteenth Century England', *Sociology*, vol. 3, no. 3, September 1974.

Johnson, T., *Professions and Power*, Macmillan, London, 1972.

Kerr, J.M. (ed.), *Historical Review of British Obstetrics and Gynaecology 1800-1950*, Livingstone, London, 1954.

Kerr, J.M., 'Notable Advances 1800-1850' in J.M. Kerr, op. cit., 1954.

King, L.S., *Medical World of the Eighteenth Century*, Robert E. Krieger Publishing Co. Inc., 1971.

London Medical Directory, C. Mitchell, London, 1845.

McKeown T., and Brown, R.G., 'Medical Evidence Related to English Population Changes in the Eighteenth Century', *Population Studies*, vol. IX, 1955.

Maitland, W., *The History of London from its foundation to the present time*, new edn continued to the year 1772 by Rev. John Entick, J. Wilkie, London, 1775.

Marshall, D., *English Poor in the Eighteenth Century*, George Routledge & Sons, London, 1962.

Maubray, J., *The Female Physician containing all the diseases incident to the sex . . . To which is added the whole art of midwifery*, London, 1724.

Munk, W., *Roll of the Royal College of Physicians of London*, vol. II, 1701-1800, Longman, London, 1861.

Nicholls, F., *The petition of the unborn babes to the censors of the Royal College of Physicians of London*, 2nd edn, Cooper, London, 1751.

Nihell, E., *A Treatise on the Art of Midwifery setting forth various abuses therein especially as to practice with instruments . . . upon the question which is it best to employ, in cases of pregnancy and lying in, a man-midwife or a midwife*, London, 1760.

Parry, N. and J., *The Rise of the Medical Profession*, Croom Helm, 1976.

Pugh, B., *A Treatise of Midwifery, chiefly with regard to the operation with several improvements in the art*, London, 1754.

Radcliffe, W., *The Secret Instrument*, Heinemann, London, 1947.

Radcliffe, W., *Milestones in Midwifery*, John Wright, Bristol, 1967.

Select Committee on Medical Education, Report and Proceeding, 1834.

Smellie, W., *A Treatise on the Theory and Practice of Midwifery*, London, 1752.

Thicknesse, P., *Letter to a Young Lady*, London, 1764.

Thicknesse, P., *Man-Midwifery Analyzed and the Tendency of that Practice Detected and Exposed*, London, 1764.

Ward, E., *The Whole Pleasures of Matrimony*, London, 1710.

Woodward, J.H., *To do the sick no harm: a Study of the British Voluntary Hospital System to 1875*, Routledge & Kegan Paul, 1974.

3

Competing ideologies of reproduction: medical and maternal perspectives on pregnancy

Hilary Graham and *Ann Oakley*

In recent years, women's experiences of childbearing have become a focus of public debate. Criticisms of maternity care (Association for Improvement in the Maternity Services, 1970; Fleury, 1967; Rathbone, 1973; Royal College of Midwives, 1966) have been countered by medical contentions that dissatisfaction is confined to a minority of middle-class patients and that most women are satisfied (Chalmers, 1976; BMJ, 1975). However, the findings from a number of recent investigations challenge the medical perspective, suggesting instead that conflict, rather than being a peripheral issue, is in fact a fundamental feature of the relationship between the providers and users of the maternity services. Some investigations have explored the ambiguity and conflict surrounding particular aspects of modern obstetrical practice, for example the question of home confinements and induction,[1] while other studies have pointed to differences in lay and medical perspectives which underlie these particular areas of controversy. These two perspectives have been identified in studies of women's experiences of maternity care, on the one hand, and in studies of the organisation of antenatal care, on the other.[2] In this chapter, Hilary Graham and Ann Oakley approach the question of what have been called 'the conflicting paradigms of pregnancy' (Comaroff, 1977) in a different way.[3] *Rather than concentrating on one particular perspective, they look at the areas of conflict which emerge when user and provider meet. In their first section, Graham and Oakley contrast perspectives held by patients and by one group of professionals involved in antenatal care – the doctors – and suggest reasons for the divergences. Second, they illustrate the way these competing perspectives influence interaction between women and doctors, both distorting and hindering communication in antenatal consultations. The emphasis in this chapter is on doctors rather than midwives or any other group of professionals for two reasons. In the first place, as Margaret Versluysen shows in her contribution, the way in which reproductive care has evolved in Britain and in western countries generally since the eighteenth century has placed control over the structure and content of care in the hands of doctors, increasingly relegating the midwife to the role of obstetric nurse. Second, the data themselves on which Graham and Oakley draw, focus on the relationship between patient and doctor. By selecting doctors rather than midwives in this way, the authors do not themselves intend to relegate the midwife to an inferior role, and indeed would want to point out that the midwife's role in contemporary medical care is a subject on which research is urgently needed (Walker, 1972, 1976).*

In talking about the different ways in which doctors and mothers view pregnancy, we are talking about a fundamental difference in their perspectives on the meaning of childbearing. It is not simply a difference of opinion about approach and procedures – about whether pregnancy is normal or pathological, or whether or not labour should be routinely induced. Rather, we are suggesting that doctors and mothers have a qualitatively different way of looking at the nature, context and management of reproduction. In this chapter, we use the concept of a frame of reference to indicate this difference. 'Frame of reference' embraces both the notion of an ideological perspective – a system of values and attitudes through which mothers and doctors view pregnancy – and of a reference group – a network of individuals who are significant influences upon these sets of attitudes and values.

We will first of all describe the main features of the two frames of reference and then go on to discuss some of the ways in which differences between them are displayed in antenatal consultations and in women's experiences of having a baby.

Obstetricians and mothers: contrasts in their frame of reference

The differences in the two frames of reference revolved around divergent views of both the nature of childbearing and the context in which it is seen. Specifically, our data suggest that mothers and doctors disagree on whether pregnancy is a natural or a medical process and whether, as a consequence, pregnancy should be abstracted from the woman's life-experiences and treated as an isolated medical event. These two issues are in turn related to two other areas of disagreement. The first concerns the way the quality of childbearing is assessed – in other words what are the criteria of success? The second concerns the way the quality of reproduction is ensured, i.e. who controls childbearing? It is these four issues (what is the nature and context of reproduction, how is success measured and how is it controlled) that lie at the heart of the conflict between mothers' and doctors' frames of reference. Anthropologists have discussed questions about the nature, context and control of childbearing in describing the differences in the management of childbirth between Western and non-Western cultures (Mead and Newton 1967; Mnecke, 1976; Oakley, 1977). The issues of nature, context and control have also been identified as crucial to an understanding of the historical development of Western obstetrics (Oakley, 1976). Interestingly, these dimensions have been less systematically explored in the study of the structure and processes of modern maternity care.

Nature of childbearing

Obstetricians

The key element in the doctor's perspective on reproduction is the status of reproduction as a medical subject. Pregnancy and birth are analogous to other physiological processes as topics of medical knowledge and treatment. The association of obstetrics with gynaecology as a specialism reinforces this lack of distinction between reproduction and the rest of medicine, by setting aside a special area to do with the physiological attributes of womanhood (Fleury, 1967; Rathbone, 1973; Scully and Bart, 1973).

Mothers

Bearing children is seen by mothers to be a natural biological process. It is akin to other biological processes (like menstruation) that occur in a woman's life. This is not to say that it is a woman's 'natural destiny' to bear children. Rather, for those women who do, the process is rooted in their bodies and in their lives and not in a medical textbook (Graham, 1977).

Context of childbearing

Obstetricians

The obstetrician's frame of reference attaches a particular, and a limited, significance to pregnancy and birth as medical events. The doctor views the individual's career as a pregnant and parturient woman as an isolated patient-episode. Pregnancy means entry into medical care as an antenatal patient, and the end of pregnancy, marked by discharge from maternity care, is the termination of this career. Being a patient is the woman's key status so far as the obstetrician is concerned, although other statuses she might have, for example as an unmarried person, as an engineer or street-cleaner, may affect the doctor's attitudes and behaviour *vis-à-vis* the patient by influencing his/her perception of the kind of medical treatment and patient-communication that is most appropriate (Stoller Shaw, 1974; Macintyre, 1976; Aitken Swan, 1977).

Mothers

A woman views reproduction not as an isolated episode of medical treatment but as an event which is integrated with other aspects of her life. Having a baby affects not only her medical status, it has implications for most of her other social roles. This is seen most clearly during first pregnancy and birth when a woman becomes a mother – that is, she acquires a new social role. But even in subsequent births, her role can change as her pregnancy affects her occupational standing, her financial position, her housing situation, her marital status and her personal relationships. As Hart (1977) has shown the new baby impinges permanently and comprehensively on a woman's life-style.

Criteria of success

Obstetricians

The obstetrician's frame of reference gives a particular and again restricted meaning to the notion of 'successful' reproduction. Here the reference point is perinatal and maternal mortality rates, and to a lesser degree certain restricted indices of morbidity. A 'successful' pregnancy is one which results in a physically healthy baby and mother as assessed in the period immediately following birth, i.e. while mother and child are still under the obstetrician's care (Haire 1972; Richards 1974).

Mothers

Because of the holistic way in which women view childbearing, the notion of successful reproduction is considerably more complex than the simple measurement of mortality and morbidity. Though in almost all cases the goal of the live birth of a healthy infant is paramount, success means primarily a satisfactory personal experience. This applies not only to the pregnancy and birth but to the subsequent mother-baby relationship and to the way in which motherhood is integrated with the rest of a woman's life. Unlike the obstetrician's criteria of success, these criteria – pregnancy/birth experiences, experiences with the mother-baby relationship, and experiences with integrating motherhood into a woman's life-style – are not separable or easily observable, but can only be assessed in the weeks, months or even years following birth (Kitzinger, 1972).

Control of childbearing

Obstetricians

The medical frame of reference defines reproduction as a specialist subject in which obstetricians are the experts, possessing (by virtue of their training) greater expertise than any other social group. This expertise is not limited to any one particular area, for example, the mechanics of the birth process, but is held to extend to the entire symptomatology of childbearing (Scully and Bart, op. cit.; Kaiser and Kaiser, 1974).

Mothers

Mothers view themselves as knowledgeable about pregnancy and birth. This knowledge stems not primarily from medical science, but rather from a woman's capacity to sense and respond to the sensations of her body. Rather than being an abstract knowledge acquired through formal training, it is thus an individualised and to some extent intuitive knowledge built up from bodily experiences (Boyle 1975; Goldthorpe and Richman 1976; McKinlay 1973).

Conflicts in the frames of reference

How do the conflicts we have seen between medical and maternal frames of reference manifest themselves? In trying to explain this, we concentrate on data relating to interaction in the antenatal clinic as this is the main forum in which mothers and medics meet. We have selected dimensions of doctor-patient interaction which illustrate and substantiate the differences between doctors and mothers already identified. These four dimensions are: (1) conflict over the status of reproduction as health or illness; (2) the question of the doctor-as-expert versus the mother-as-expert; (3) the issue of who makes the decisions about reproductive care; and (4) the kind of communication doctors and mothers see as appropriate to their joint interaction.

Health or illness?

One important norm within the culture of the medical profession is that judging a sick person well is more to be avoided than judging a well person sick. This 'medical decision rule' is applied to obstetrics as it is to other branches of medicine; every pregnancy and labour is treated as though it is, or could be, abnormal, and the weight of the obstetrician's medical education acts against his/her achievement of work-satisfaction in the treatment of unproblematic reproduction (Scheff, 1963). The 'as if ill' role was a recurrent feature in the observed interactions between doctors and patients. It was made explicit when doctors needed to explain or justify particular medical attitudes and routines to their patients. Such explanations and justifications might be called for when a doctor discussed the type of antenatal care he/she felt most appropriate for his patient, when advising on a woman's employment and domestic commitment or when prescribing medical treatment.[4] For example:

Patient: I'm a hairdresser. I only do three days a week – is it all right to go on working?

Doctor: Up to twenty-eight weeks is all right on the whole, especially if you have a trouble-free pregnancy as you obviously have. After that it's better to give up.
Patient: I only work three days a week, I feel fine.
Doctor: Yes, everything *is* fine, but now you've got to this stage it's better to give up, just in case.

But the most common way in which the 'as if ill' rule is manifested in antenatal care today is through the routine prescription of various tests and procedures such as ultrasonic scanning, twenty-four hour urine collection for the measurement of placental function, and frequent internal examination to assess the competence of the cervix. The subject of tests and procedures occupies an important place in the antenatal encounter. In nearly half the encounters observed in the London hospital, there was at least one reference to technology – to one testing procedure or another. Of the questions asked by patients, 29 per cent concerned medical technology – ultrasound, blood tests, induction and so on, and another 5 per cent concerned prescribed drugs. For some women these sophisticated procedures and forms of treatment are the hallmark of a 'proper' pregnancy. Other women felt less happy about this medicalisation of childbearing, unaware perhaps of the equation between pregnancy and illness until they began their careers as antenatal patients. The first antenatal visit thus comes as a considerable shock, disturbing long-held notions about pregnancy as a natural process. One London mother put the case succinctly:

> 'I thought, okay, first baby, the best thing to do is to have it in hospital, because it's far more of an unknown quantity . . . but it's this concern with medicine that seems to override everything else – the natural process, I mean. I mean it is something that women have always been brought up to do; everybody knows that, okay, it's painful, having labour and everything, but it's very rewarding; it's the one pain we've been brought up to expect and not to be scared of. Before the hospital

thing pregnancy was a normal, nice condition. I'm not sure it isn't an illness now.'

Apprehension about medicalised reproduction is greatest among primiparae (first-time mothers), two-thirds of whom expressed anxiety about antenatal checkups. The focus of this anxiety is often the vaginal examination, and, for more than half of the York and London primiparae, this was their first experience of this examination.

> 'I'll tell you what terrified me, the internal, cos I'd never had one before and the very thought of it, oh God! For a week I was so nervous, I thought I'd get desperate diarrhoea, I was all colly wobbles and I was like that for a whole week.'

The vaginal examination is of course an important part of antenatal work. Of the encounters observed in the London hospital, 28 per cent included an internal examination but rarely was the medical rationale for the examination made explicit. Again, the 'as if ill' rule is rarely articulated by medical staff unless a procedure or a prescription is questioned or challenged by a patient. This is illustrated in the following consultation, where a patient refuses an internal examination. She has had a previous termination and her cervix is being assessed fortnightly as part of a research project designed to see whether regular internal examinations are of any use in preventing abortion due to cervical incompetence. On this occasion she refuses the examination and the doctor asks why:

Patient: The doctor last time, he hurt me, and I had a lot of bleeding afterwards – he promised he wouldn't do it again.

Doctor: I don't care a damn what the doctor promised last time. If you lose the baby it's up to you. Do you know why we do these examinations?

Patient: I thought it was to tell the size of the baby.

Doctor: No, it's nothing to do with that. You've had a termination and this can cause prematurity, and we look to see if the womb is opening up. If it is, we put a stitch in.

The purpose of the regular internal examinations had clearly not been explained to the patient – until she challenged medical dictate.

Who is the expert?

A second way in which the differences between doctors' and mothers' frames of reference is manifested is in conflicts over expertise: in conflicts between doctor-as-expert and mother-as-expert. The definition and interpretation of significant symptoms was a common area of divergence between mothers and doctors. To the doctor, symptoms of importance are those that betray the patient's clinical condition: swollen fingers or ankles, blurred vision, bleeding and so forth. But the patient may very often report symptoms which worry her but which do not worry the doctor. She is reacting to her subjective experience of pregnancy, to her feelings about the physical and emotional changes that pregnancy has brought about. For example:

Patient: I get pains in my groin, down here, why is that?
Doctor: Well, it's some time since your last pregnancy, and also your centre of gravity is changing.
Patient: I see.
Doctor: That's okay. (Pats on back.)

Since it is often possible from the patient's account for the doctor to assess the clinical significance of the symptom, the patient's statement of pain may be ignored or dismissed in a joking manner.

Patient: I've got a pain in my shoulder.
Doctor: Well, that's your shopping bag hand, isn't it?

Differences in symptom-description are of course a general characteristic of doctor-patient interaction (Stimson and

Webb, 1975). This kind of medical response which may evoke considerable anxiety in the patient was far from rare: of the 677 statements made by patients during the series of antenatal clinic encounters observed in London, 12 per cent concerned symptoms of pain or discomfort which the doctor ignored or dismissed as clinically unimportant. Mothers also state their feelings about the pregnancy and the birth, sometimes relating these to their social circumstances – a bad marriage, poor housing, for instance and 8 per cent of the statements made by patients were of this kind. Very rarely did the doctor respond seriously to such statements:

Patient: My doctor gave me some tablets for vomiting earlier on but I was reluctant to take them.
Doctor: Are you still reluctant?
Patient: Well I feel so depressed, I'm so fed up. . . .
Doctor: (interrupting) Shall I give you some tablets for vomiting?

Mothers' and doctors' different fields of expertise also compete over the dating of the pregnancy. In the London hospital, as in others, the date of the patient's last menstrual period is asked for routinely on booking-in at the clinic and the time at which foetal movements are first felt is also requested. The routinisation of these questions acknowledges their importance, but medical attitudes to the reliability of women's information on these points tend to be sceptical. For example:

Doctor: How many weeks are you now?
Patient: Twenty-six-and-a-half.
Doctor: (looking at case notes) Twenty weeks now.
Patient. No, twenty-six-and-a-half.
Doctor: You can't be.
Patient: Yes, I am; look at the ultrasound report.
Doctor: When was it done?
Patient: Today.
Doctor: It was done today?
Patient: Yes.

Doctor: (reads report) Oh yes, twenty-six-and-a-half weeks, that's right.

Perhaps it is significant that increasingly the routine use of ultrasound is providing an alternative medical technique for the assessment of gestation length; a medical rationale for the inflation of medical over maternal expertise is thus provided. During consultations in the London antenatal clinic, 6 per cent of the questions asked and 5 per cent of the statements made by mothers concerned dates, mothers usually trying to negotiate the 'correct' date of expected delivery with the doctor who did not see this as a subject for negotiation or as a legitimate area of maternal expertise.

Who controls reproduction?

The women interviewed both in York and London reported very few areas in which they were able to exercise choicc about the kind of maternity care they had. From the moment they first saw a doctor about the pregnancy, decisions were made for them. As one mother in York put it:

> 'Well, when I went to see my doctor, he's ever so nice, he said he advised me to have it in hospital. I'm more or less putting my foot down, he said, that you have it in hospital. So I really didn't have any choice.'

This lack of control experienced by mothers extended right through their antenatal careers. One sign of mothers' desires to feel in control of their reproductive care is the number of questions they ask about the progress of their pregnancy. Of all questions asked in the London antenatal clinic, 20 per cent concerned the size or position of the baby, foetal heart sounds, maternal weight and blood pressure. A further 20 per cent were questions about the physiology of pregnancy and birth in general or about related medical procedures. These are serious requests but are often casually treated by doctors with resulting confusion and anxiety in the mother.

Actual conflict between mother and doctor over medical decisions was rare in the research series, but it did characterise some encounters, and was particularly likely to do so when decisions about delivery were being made. These confrontations between mothers and doctors thus illustrate one way in which some women express a desire to control what happens to them in childbirth.

A registrar, examining a woman towards the end of her first pregnancy, does an internal examination and comments:

Doctor: It'd be difficult to get you off now – I think you ought to come in for the rest and to do some more water tests and then we can start you off. The baby isn't growing as fast as it was.

Patient: What do you mean, come in?

Doctor: Really it's a matter of when you come in, Sunday, I should think, and then stay in.

Patient: Stay in until it's born, you mean.

Doctor: Yes.

Patient: I don't fancy that very much.

Doctor: If you'd been ready I would have started you off today. You see on the ultrasound it's not growing as well as it was, and on the water tests the oestriols are falling – it's not bad, but you should come in and have some water tests, get some rest, and then we can start you off sometime next week probably, when you're ready.

Patient: If my husband wanted to come and talk to you about inducing me, can I make an appointment for him?

Doctor: I don't think anything your husband said would affect our decision one way or the other.

Patient: No, but he would like to talk to you.

Doctor: Yes, well he can talk to whoever's on duty, but there's nothing he can say that will affect us: it's a medical question.

Patient: Yes, but he'd still like to talk it over, find out what's going on.

Doctor: What it amounts to is that we won't be browbeaten by the *Sunday Times*.[5]

Patient: No, I understand that.

Doctor: If we explained to everyone, and everyone's husband, we'd spend all our time explaining. *I think you've got to assume if you come here for medical attention that we make all the decisions*. In fact I think you should come in today, but I've already been browbeaten into saying Sunday, which is another forty-eight hours.

Here the doctor refuses to 'discuss' the proposed induction with the patient, taking it as axiomatic that the most that should be expected of him is an explanation of the reasons why he wants to induce labour. Interestingly, cases in the series where patients objected to induction all met with hostility from the doctor, whereas when the patient either explicitly or implicitly requested an induction this met with a very different response: in some cases the patient's request was granted, but even where it was not, the plea for induction was accepted as legitimate patient-behaviour. In asking for an induction the patient is subscribing to two important norms in obstetric treatment: the idea that technological childbirth is 'good' childbirth, and the notion that while the doctor's superior expertise may be challenged by *refusing* medical decisions, it is *confirmed* by polite requests for them; 'begging for mercy' is how the doctors often described such requests.

The communication gap

Problems in communicating with doctors were commonly reported in both York and London. Mothers' comments pick out the following related themes:[6]

(a) not feeling able to ask questions;
(b) not having sufficient explanation of medical treatment or the progress of the pregnancy from the doctor;
(c) being treated as ignorant;
(d) seeing too many different doctors;
(e) feeling rushed, like 'battery hens', animals in a 'cattle

market' or items on a 'conveyor belt' or an 'assembly line'.

Asking questions

In the London hospital observations, questions asked by patients averaged slightly more than 1 per encounter and statements made by patients (i.e. not in response to anything the doctor said) slightly less. Of the women interviewed in York, 80 per cent said that they had learnt nothing from their antenatal checkups; 40 per cent felt they couldn't ask questions – and of those who did feel they could in theory, many didn't in practice:

> 'The nurse says "now do you want to ask the doctor anything?" And more invariably than not you say "no" because you just don't feel you can. The way they ask you, "Right, do you want to ask the doctor anything?" you think, no. All you want to do is get up and get out.'

Getting explanations

When mothers do ask questions they usually require much fuller information than the medical staff are prepared to give. A quick 'that's normal' or 'that's nothing to worry about' is not sufficient. Take the disquiet experienced by one London mother:

> 'I've been getting really bad stomach pains like I'm coming on. I said that to the doctor – I said I had bad stomach pains, he said it's usual but I mean they're getting worse. I said I'm getting pains like I'm coming on. He said you do get this. But they're getting worse. It might *be* usual, but. . . . '

Being treated as ignorant

These complaints relate to medical definitions of mothers as ignorant about medical aspects of pregnancy. One York mother, worried about contact with rubella, said:

'I mean you don't need to have done midwifery to know the complications and I wanted an answer. I think my own GP sent my blood off on the Friday and this was Tuesday or Wednesday so I knew the results were there [at the clinic]. But, "Oh you might hear in the next few days"; it wasn't good enough for me, every hour I was thinking about it. . . . Some nurses and doctors are terribly condescending. And this girl irritated me, so I said, "When will I know the results of this rubella test?" "It's out of your hands now, deary, the doctor knows all about it" and I did feel very irritated by that, I'm an intelligent woman and it annoyed me.'

The assumption of ignorance may be a common component in doctors' attitudes to patients (Kaiser and Kaiser, op. cit.; Davis and Horobin, 1977) but patients in antenatal clinics are always women and the doctors are predominantly men[7] (Ehrenreich, 1974). Typifications of women as women are certainly articulated in antenatal consultations; for example:[8]

Doctor: How many babies have you got?
Patient: This is the third pregnancy.
Doctor: Doing your duty, aren't you?

Or:

Doctor: This is twins . . . they're growing well, but you need more rest . . . I'd advise some good books and a quiet life for three months. You're not working.
Patient: No.
Doctor: Just normal exercise – I want you to have a walk every day, but no gardening, no heavy work, postpone moving or decorating the house. If you do rest, you'll grow yourself slightly bigger babies. After all, it's this (pats her abdomen) that's your most important job isn't it?

And women, it is implied, are inherently unreliable sources

of information:

Doctor: (reading case notes) Ah, I see you've got a boy and a girl.
Patient: No, two girls.
Doctor: Really. Are you sure? I thought it said . . . [checks in notes] oh no, you're quite right, two girls.

Or:

Doctor: Are you absolutely sure of your dates?
Patient: Yes, and I can even tell you the date of conception. (Doctor laughs) No, I'm serious, this is an artificial insemination baby. (The husband is a paraplegic, and the patient's previous child was also born as a result of artificial insemination.)

Seeing different doctors

The problem of unsatisfactory communication with doctors is compounded by seeing a different face at every clinic visit. One London mother describes her experience:

> 'The thing is you get such *varied* opinions – one of them says about your weight and the next time you go I think this is it: I'm going to be told off about my weight again, and then I go and I see somebody completely different and nobody says a thing about it . . . I come out feeling completely confused.'

In the York sample, 81 per cent of mothers said they would prefer to see the same doctor every time.

Being on a conveyor belt

All these communication difficulties are related to the organisation of antenatal clinics which tend to resemble assembly lines, if only because a small number of doctors must see a large number of patients in a short space of time. In the London antenatal clinic the average time per doctor-patient encounter was 3.9 minutes. It is rarely possible within this framework for mothers to feel that they have been treated as individuals or that they have had a 'good' experience – and such is the emotional meaning of pregnancy to women that many have high expectations of their maternity care. A York mother:

> 'You sort of feel I've waited all the time, and you're just sat there . . . and I don't know, they treat you like you were just an animal, and yet it's a big thing to you. The first time in nineteen years that something happens, it's a new experience to you although it may be everyday to them. Some of them just don't realise this.'

Of all statements made by patients in the London antenatal clinic, 8 per cent were statements of worry or anxiety reflecting dissatisfaction with the kind of communication offered by doctors. Another symptom of patient dissatisfaction is the unanswered (or unasked) question that is posed to the researcher. Indeed in the London project this was a frequent theme of the interviews. Sometimes the unanswered question is a very basic one and a source of great worry to the mother:

Researcher: Did you ask any questions?

Patient: No I didn't. You see when it comes to that I'm very shy in asking questions.

Researcher: Did you want to ask any questions?

Patient: Yes. Is it dangerous like? Can anything happen to you? That's the most I think I wanted to ask. I'm very frightened. I just pray. They asked me – 'any questions?' I just said no. I'm frightened if anything will happen. You know a lot of people in Ireland they used to die having children. . . . There's one question I'm very worried about. And I didn't like to ask it. Since I got pregnant I can't have intercourse at all. I just can't. I don't know why. It hurts. I just can't have it. . . . Is it natural, I wonder? I've got a little baby book there and

> it says in that book that you should have no problem. It says you should have intercourse with your husband up until seven or eight months.

Patients' difficulties in communicating with doctors are rooted in medical definitions of the ideal mode of interaction with patients in which patient-passivity is central; the patient asks no questions and co-operates with the doctor in all the procedures defined medically as necessary. For example:

Doctor: (entering cubicle) Hello.
Patient: Hello.
Doctor: (reading notes) Mrs Watkins?
Patient: Yes.
Doctor: Well, how are you?
Patient: Fine, thank you.
Doctor: Can I feel your tummy? (He undoes the buttons on her dressing gown and does so.) Any complaints?
Patient: No.
Doctor: (filling in notes) Have you felt the baby move yet?
Patient: Yes.
Doctor: How long have you felt it?
Patient: Two weeks.
Doctor: (feels patient's ankles) All the tests we did last time were good.
Patient: Good.
Doctor: Okay. (Leaves cubicle.)

This mode of interaction is facilitated by the layout of many antenatal clinics, including those described by women in the York and London research projects. A cubicle system for examining patients, and the requirement that patients lie on couches ready for the doctor, militate against doctor-patient interaction as equals. In the London hospital, patients who were found by doctors sitting rather than lying on the couch were degarded as deviant; significantly, patients who began their medical encounters in this way asked more questions and were given more time by the doctor.

The most typical way in which doctors themselves exceed the kind of minimal interaction demanded by the passive-patient model is by offering certain restricted kinds of explanation to the patient. The subject of the doctor's explanation may be the physiology of pregnancy, clinic procedure or the technology of ultrasound. Particular kinds of language are used in these explanations.[9] Technical language in explanations is reserved for cases where a doctor wants to encourage a patient to agree to a particular procedure (and perceives her as unwilling to do so). Thus, in the example quoted earlier of a conflict over induction, the doctor referred to 'oestriol' tests as 'water' tests until the patient expressed hostility to the idea of intervention in her pregnancy, at which point he informed her that 'the oestriols are falling'. For other types of explanation, a form of 'lay' language is used. Examples are 'tail', 'feeling inside', 'start you off' (for induction) and terms such as 'tickling' and 'stirring up' for sweeping the membranes as a covert method of inducing labour. This lay language seems to be used fairly indiscriminately, although the doctor's perception of the social class or medical status of the patient may affect his/her choice of words. Thus one houseman regularly used the phrase 'vaginal examination' for patients with middle-class occupations, reserving the phrase 'examine you down below' for those whom he saw as working class.

In addition to this dependence on a form of lay language, the doctor also trivialises and is deliberately non-specific in his description of medical procedures. A thorough and probably uncomfortable internal examination may be trivialised to become 'a little examination' or 'a gentle examination'; induction may be given the label 'a push downhill' or 'marching orders'. For example, one patient asked, 'What do they usually do when they start you off; my last baby I had normally?' The doctor replied, 'It's nothing terrible. They do an internal and break the waters and then drip some magic stuff into your arm.' Such 'explanations' are based on an underlying typification of patients as anxious. Indeed, there seemed to be a widespread supposition among the doctors observed that the reason patients asked questions was anxiety and that, therefore, the main aim of medical explanations was to allay anxiety (rather than to give information). As the following exchange shows, joking is often used as a device for supposedly reducing patient-anxiety, although, as we have seen, it does not necessarily do so:

First Doctor: You're looking serious.
Patient: Well, I am rather worried about it all. It feels like a small baby – I feel much smaller with this one than I did with my first, and she weighed under six pounds. Ultrasound last week said the baby was very small as well.
First doctor: Weighed it, did they?
Second doctor: (entering examination cubicle) They go round to flower shows and weigh cakes, you know.
First doctor: Yes, it's a piece of cake really.

We have briefly outlined here some of the main features of medical and maternal perspectives on pregnancy and birth which emerged during two research projects. We have attempted to 'explain' certain conflicts between the two perspectives by rooting these conflicts in the particular frames of reference employed by the providers and users of maternity care. The frames of reference have been described primarily in terms of the differing social positions and perspectives of these two groups as they interact as *doctors* and *patients*. In outlining these conflicts in present-day maternity care, we have left unanswered the crucial question of what should be done. There appear to be two basic kinds of solution available – one which works within the existing organisation of maternity care, the other which involves working towards alternative patterns of care. The first type of solution would involve, for example, redesigning antenatal clinics so that the sense of rush and anonymity is minimised, educating doctors to be less dogmatic about the 'needs' of maternity patients, and encouraging mothers to be more articulate and more reasonable about the kind of maternity care they want. But more fundamental changes may be felt to be necessary to ameliorate the conflicts between doctors and mothers. It may be that changes *of* the system itself, rather than changes *in* the system are required. Such changes might entail the development of neighbourhood maternity centres, a move back towards home delivery, a transfer of medical responsibility from doctors to midwives, and less task-oriented and more patient-oriented maternity care.

Notes

1 Such work includes studies by Kitzinger, 1975; Cartwright, 1977; Royal College of Obstetricians and Gynaecologists, 1975; Goldthorpe and Richman, 1974; and O'Brien, 1977.

2 Comaroff (1977), Hart (1977), Oakley (1975), and Graham (1976) have produced writings on the former, Macintyre (1976) on the latter.

3 The background to the paper consists of two research projects, one undertaken in the Social Research Unit of Bedford College, University of London, by Ann Oakley, and funded by the Social Science Research Council; the other in the Department of Sociology, University of York, by Hilary Graham and Lorna McKee, and funded by the Health Education Council. Both projects are concerned with women's experiences of pregnancy, childbearing and the early post-natal period. In addition, the London project included a period of six months' observation of staff-patient interaction in a maternity hospital. Both the projects have uncovered a substantial amount of data relating to both users' and providers' views on how the maternity services do, and should operate. Although the studies cover two different geographical areas and two different hospitals – a small provincial and a large metropolitan one – the two projects point to basic similarities in attitudes and experiences.

4 Maternal employment *per se* is of course not related to reproductive causality, although other variables that are associated with it, for instance low socio-economic status, do show some such relationship (Illsley, 1967).

5 The doctor is referring to two articles written by L. Gillie and O. Gillie (1974) in the *Sunday Times*.

6 It is interesting to note the similarity between these themes and those picked out in the Standing Maternity and Midwifery Advisory Committee document *Human Relations and Obstetrics*, HMSO, 1961.

7 In September 1977, 25.4 per cent of the gynaecologists and obstetricians in England and Wales listed as hospital medical

staff by the DHSS were women (DHSS, 1978).

8 A similar pattern of attitudes and treatment regarding female patients has been found outside gynaecology and obstetrics. See Barrett and Roberts (1978).

9 Emerson (1970) has described the medical language used in vaginal examinations.

References

Aitken Swan, J. (1977), *Fertility Control and the Medical Profession*, Croom Helm, London.

Association for Improvement in the Maternity Services (1970), *Survey of the Opinions of Mothers on the Maternity Services in England and Wales*, King Edward's Hospital Fund for London.

Barrett, M., and Roberts, H. (1978), 'Doctors and their Patients: the Social control of women in general practice', in C. Smart and B. Smart (eds), *Women, Sexuality and Social Control*, Routledge & Kegan Paul, London.

Boyle, C.M. (1975), 'Differences between Patients' and Doctors' Interpretations of Some Common Medical Terms', in C. Cox, and A. Mead (eds), *A Sociology of Medical Practice*, Collier Macmillan, London.

British Medical Journal (1975), editorial, vol. 539, no. 1.

Cartwright, A. (1977), 'Mothers' Experiences of Induction', in *British Medical Journal*, 17 September.

Chalmers, I. (1976), 'British Debate on Obstetric Practice', *Pediatrics*, no. 3, pp. 308-12.

Comaroff, J. (1977), 'Conflicting Paradigms of Pregnancy: Managing Ambiguity in Antenatal Encounters', in A. Davis and G. Horobin (eds), *Medical Encounters: Experience of Illness and Treatment*, Croom Helm, London.

Davis, A., and Horobin, G. (eds) (1977), *Medical Encounters: Experience of Illness and Treatment*, Croom Helm, London.

Donnison, J. (1977), *Midwives and Medical Men*, Heinemann, London.

Ehrenreich, B. (1974), 'Gender and Objectivity in Medicine', *International Journal of Health Services*, vol. 4, p. 617.

Emerson, J. (1970), 'Behaviour in Private Places: Sustaining Definitions of Reality in Gynaecological Examinations', in H.P. Dreitzel, (ed), *Recent Sociology*, no. 2, Macmillan, New York.

Fleury, P.M. (1967), *Maternity Care: Mother's Experiences of Childbirth*, Allen & Unwin, London.

Gillie, L., and Gillie, O. (1974), *Sunday Times*, 13 and 20 October.

Goldthorpe, W.O., and Richman, J. (1974), 'Maternal Attitudes to Unintended Home Confinement', *Practitioner*, no. 212, p. 845.

Goldthorpe, W.O., and Richman, J. (1975, 1976), 'The Gynaecological Patient's Knowledge of her Illness and Treatment', *British Journal of Sexual Medicine*, December 1975 and February 1976.

Graham, H. (1976), 'The Social Image of Pregnancy: Pregnancy as Spirit Possession', *Sociological Review*, vol. 24, p. 291.

Graham, H. (1977), 'Women's Attitudes to Conception and Pregnancy', in R. Chester and J. Peel (eds), *Equalities and Inequalities in Family Life*, Academic Press, London.

Haire, D. (1972), *The Cultural Warping of Childbirth*, International Childbirth Education Association News.

Hart, N. (1977), *'Technology and Childbirth – a Dialectical Autobiography'*, in A. Davis and G. Horobin, op. cit.

Illsley, R. (1967), 'The Sociological Study of Reproduction and its Outcome', in S.A. Richardson and A.F. Guttmacher (eds), *Childbearing: its Social and Psychological Aspects*, Williams & Wilkins, Baltimore.

Kaiser, B.L., and Kaiser, I.H. (1974), 'The Challenge of the Women's Movement to American Gynaecology', *American Journal of Obstetrics and Gynaecology*, pp. 652-65.

Kitzinger, S. (1972), *The Experience of Childbirth*, Penguin, Harmondsworth.

Kitzinger, S. (1975), *Some Mothers' Experiences of Induced Labour*, National Childbirth Trust, London.

Macintyre, S. (1976), 'Who Wants Babies? The Social Construction of Instincts', in D. Barker and S. Allen (eds), *Sexual Divisions and Society: Process and Change*, Tavistock, London.

Macintyre, S. (1976), 'Obstetric Routines in Antenatal Care', paper given at the British Sociological Association Medical Sociology Conference, York.

McKinlay, J. (1973), 'Social Networks, Lay Consultation and Help-Seeking Behaviour', *Social Forces*, no. 51, pp. 275-92.

Mead, M., and Newton, N. (1967), 'Cultural Patterning of Perinatal Behaviour', in S. Richardson and A. Guttmacher, op. cit.

Mnecke, M.A. (1976), 'Health Care Systems as Socialising Agents: Childbearing the North Thai and Western Ways', *Social Science and Medicine*, no. 10, pp. 377-83.

Oakley, A. (1975), 'The Trap of Medicalised Motherhood', *New Society*, vol. 34, p. 639.

Oakley, A. (1976), 'Wisewoman and Medicine Man: Changes in the Management of Childbirth', in J. Mitchell and A. Oakley (eds), *The Rights and Wrongs of Women*, Penguin, Harmondsworth.

Oakley, A. (1977), 'Cross Cultural Practice', in T. Chard and M. Richards (eds), *Benefits and Hazards of the New Obstetrics*, Heinemann, London.

O'Brien, M. (1977), 'Home and Hospital: a Comparison of the Experiences of Mothers Having Home and Hospital Confinements', paper given at the Second Seminar on Human Relations and Obstetric Practice, 30 July, University of Warwick.

Rathbone, B. (1973), *Focus on New Mothers: a Study of Antenatal*

Classes, Royal College of Nursing.
Richards, M. (1974), 'The One-Day-Old Deprived Child', *New Scientist*, 2 March, pp. 820-2.
Royal College of Midwives (1966), *Preparation for Parenthood*.
Royal College of Obstetricians and Gynaecologists (1975), *The Management of Labour*, Proceedings of Third Study Group.
Scheff, T.J. (1963), 'Decision Rules, Types of Error and Their Consequences in Medical Diagnosis', *Behavioural Science*, vol. 8, pp. 97-105.
Scully, D., and Bart, P. (1973), 'A Funny Thing Happened to Me on the Way to the Orifice: Women in Gynaecology Textbooks', *American Journal of Sociology*, vol. 78.
Stimson, G., and Webb, B. (1975), *Going to See the Doctor*, Routledge & Kegan Paul, London.
Stoller Shaw, N. (1974), *Forced Labour: Maternity Care in the United States*, Pergamon Press, New York.
Walker, J.F. (1972), 'The Changing Role of the Midwife', *International Journal of Nursing Studies*, pp. 85-94.
Walker, J.F. (1976), 'Midwife and Obstetric Nurse? Some Reflections of Midwives and Obstetricians on the Role of the Midwife', *Journal of Advanced Nursing*, vol. 1, pp. 129-38.

4

Depo-Provera: the extent of the problem A case study in the politics of birth control

Jill Rakusen

In the 1960s, the contraceptive 'pill' was seen as a great advance by women, the medical profession and those active within the family planning movement. By almost everyone, in fact, except perhaps those guardians of our morals who felt that sex without threat of 'punishment' through pregnancy would lead to all sorts of evils. It was not until the late 1960s and early 1970s when reports started coming out on possible side-effects of the pill that women began to worry – and rightly so – about the implications of taking, on a regular basis, a drug whose effects were not local but systemic.

But the problems connected with such methods of contraception go much further than an awareness and an examination of side-effects. As Helen Roberts shows in her chapter, there are numerous interests at work in the birth control empire, and the least powerful of the interest groups is that of the women using contraceptives. In this chapter, Jill Rakusen uses her work on Depo-Provera, an injectable contraceptive, as a case study in the politics of birth control. Drawing on her knowledge of the relevant literature, on cases reported to the Campaign Against Depo-Provera, and on examples drawn from her extensive interviews with social workers, community workers, and family planners, Rakusen moves between the micro and the macro, the personal and the political. At the political level, she looks at planning, research, and technology, while at the personal level, she looks at the experience of individual women. Rakusen looks at the evidence for and against Depo-Provera, examines the access (or lack of it) that women have to the relevant information, and finally suggests that it must be part of our political practice to ensure that every women is in a position to make an informed choice for herself.

This is an attempt to bring together information concerning one kind of contraceptive, information that is not normally easily available to us. By doing this, I hope first to illustrate some of the problems which we encounter when trying to evaluate medical information, second to raise questions about the kind of, and value of medical research that is performed, particularly that affecting women, and finally to look at various issues concerning the use and development of contraceptives as a whole.

At the same time, since it is so difficult for women at present to glean information about Depo-Provera, I hope that this chapter will go some way to providing a critical review of certain relevant medical research. Hopefully, this exercise will contribute to understanding some of the factors which affect women's choice and use of birth control.

Depo-Provera (DP) is an injectable contraceptive, consisting of a progestogen (meaning a synthetic form of the female hormone progesterone) called medroxyprogesterone acetate. It has an effectiveness comparable with the Pill, and it is widely used despite concern about its side-effects. The American Food and Drug Administration (FDA), in spite of repeated pressure from the manufacturers (Upjohn Co.) and the population control lobby, has refused to lift restrictions on the use of DP in the USA. The United Kingdom Committee on Safety of Medicines (CSM), taking its lead from the FDA, only licenses DP for short-term use in circumstances which fulfil two criteria: (a) where women have been immunised against rubella and need contraceptive protection for about three months, and (b) where a woman's husband has had a vasectomy and is waiting for his sperm-count to reach zero.[1]

The FDA's stance is related in part to studies where some beagle bitches who were given DP developed breast tumours, a number of which were cancerous. The FDA was sufficiently alarmed to ban *oral contraceptives* containing DP and its related compounds, chlormadinone acetate and megestrol acetate, because of similar studies on beagles. However, the injectable form of DP was allowed to remain in use as a contraceptive, as it was argued that there were no highly effective injectable alternatives.[2]

Other worrying aspects of DP include the following: there is evidence which suggests that DP might increase the risk of cervical cancer (e.g. see Powell and Seymour, 1971; and Vecchio, 1974), and there is concern about the fact that DP tends to delay the return of fertility, possibly causing permanent damage to the pituitary gland and permanent infertility in some women (e.g. Rosenfield, 1978; Apelo *et al.*, 1974; Health Research Group, 1976; Upjohn, 1972a). As the manufacturers acknowledge in their own literature, birth defects may be induced in children of women given the drug while pregnant (however, a recent review of relevant research concludes that there is as yet no convincing evidence either way), the lactation process in breast-feeding women is affected (e.g. see Parveen *at al.*, 1977; Kader *et al.*, 1975; Upjohn, 1971), and babies have been shown to absorb huge quantities of DP via their mothers' milk, to unknown effect (Saxena *et al.*, 1977). There is a suspicion that the drug could cause liver tumours (e.g. see Nissen *et al.*, 1976);[3] and, as I write, worrying evidence is beginning to emerge concerning a link between DP and endometrial cancer in monkeys (Family Planning Perspectives, 1979; and Wyrick, 1979). DP also induces symptoms in large numbers of women, which range from bleeding problems to headaches, and depression to weight gain. Some of these side-effects will be discussed in more detail below.

The 'advantage' of DP is that, by virtue of its being injectable, control need not lie in the woman's hands. It has therefore been considered particularly useful, especially in population control programmes in the Third World, and for women anywhere who 'aren't sufficiently motivated to take a pill every day[4]; cannot or *will not* use the Pill or IUD, and choose not to use condom, foam or diaphragm' (Rosenfield, 1978); who are 'unable or unwilling' to use alternatives (Smith, 1978); who are 'illiterate, unreliable or irresponsible' (Girotti and Hauser, 1970). 1978 estimates are that between three and five million women in roughly seventy countries are using DP (Corfman, 1978). The potential for the abuse of such a drug is obviously enormous.

Without doubt, the biggest potential abuse is in the Third World, where some population control programmes appear to be geared to reducing birth rates with little regard for the people at whom these programmes are directed.[5]

Reports indicate (*Business Week*, 1979) that nearly half the mothers in Africa who are using birth control currently use DP. Thousands more use it in Asia and Latin America. Aggressive policies of distributors like the International Planned Parenthood Federation (IPPF) and of Upjohn, the manufacturers, contribute to wide 'acceptance' of the drug. As Roberts points out in her chapter, it is undoubtedly the case that contraceptives are big business with an enormous potential market, and there is particular potential for aggressive marketing techniques in the Third World.

Practices are sometimes highly questionable: incentives are not uncommonly paid to family planning workers in the Third World (see, for example, First Asian Regional Workshop on Injectable Contraceptives, 1978). In a deposition to the US Securities and Exchange Commission unearthed by Minkin (1979), the manufacturers of DP admitted paying $2,710,000 in bribes to 'employees of foreign governments and to their intermediaries for the purpose of obtaining sales to government agencies'. Bribes to hospital employees raised this total to $4,098,000, and a further $147,579 was paid out 'in connection with other foreign governmental actions related to the company's business'. Upjohn's deposition specifically notes that the above figures exclude 'small amounts which were paid to minor government employees to expedite governmental services'.

The speed with which DP can be given is unashamedly regarded by population controllers as one of DP's big bonuses ('cost effectiveness' being the prime motive). This, together with DP's 'beauty' as a method of contraception that women can't control for themselves, leads to family planning workers favouring DP and its like above other methods, particularly if they are being paid incentives for 'recruits' to their programmes. In turn it leads to screening and follow-up being either cursory or non-existent (see, for example, Boston Women's Health Package, 1978).

Adequate monitoring and follow-up are uncommon for another reason, the rationale being that if they were carried out (involving, for example, pelvic examinations and cervical smears), few women would 'accept' the method (see, for example, *People*, 1975a). This desire to 'protect' women from having knowledge about, and feeling comfortable with, their own bodies is a particularly ironic aspect of the DP saga. It should also be evident that if proper screening and follow-up were practised, far fewer women would end up on DP, since speed would be lost and it would no longer be possible to treat them as if on a conveyor belt.

Given concerns for cost effectiveness, the introduction of DP has meant that other methods which are more time-consuming to fit, and dispense, start to lose favour. An open letter from an observer in Africa (Boston Women's Health Package, 1978) makes this point:

> Everyone in FP [Family Planning] seems to think that because the diaphragm requires careful fitting and inserting and needs washing and storage it is not feasible for most situations here. Most clinic workers up-country are not trained in its use; even if they were, they might well be daunted by the need to give time-consuming individual instruction. And they can't afford to provide jellies, foams, creams.

This last point illustrates how only those contraceptives which are valuable in terms of population control, as opposed to valuable as far as women's health is concerned, are considered appropriate for distribution abroad at subsidised rates.

I should add that some western medical schools today no longer teach students how to fit the diaphragm – together with the sheath, the safest method of birth control. As Dr Robert Hatcher of Emory University and Grady Memorial Hospital, Atlanta testified at the US Select Committee on Population, some doctors 'discourage diaphragms because of the time it takes to fit them properly'. As for sheaths, there is a fear in the Indian sub-continent that western rejects are commonly dumped there – which could go some way towards explaining Asian men's so-called aversion to sheaths. As one former field-worker told me, 'Out of twenty I blew up, ten were defective.'

Another reason for the undisguised pleasure with which population controllers regard DP is that, in some underdeveloped countries, injections are considered by many of the indigenous population as the best form of medicine. The population controllers build on this by fostering the belief that because DP is an injectable, it must be good.

Many abuses relating to DP centre on the question of choice and informed consent. Indeed, for a variety of reasons, few women are offered anything but a travesty of choice. I have already shown how the distributors manipulate the choices available. Depo-Provera is also associated with clear-cut coercion, as are programmes involving other 'desirable' methods such as sterilisation and IUDs (see, for example, Mass, 1976): discussing a report by a black woman (Quality of Health Care, 1973), that she was threatened – by the loss of her social security money – into accepting the drug, the director of the US National Welfare Rights Organization asserted that such cases were not uncommon (Corea, 1978). Again, it is black and minority group women who are particularly at risk from this kind of abuse.

Apart from examples of consent being sought under duress, cases have been reported where consent has not been sought at all. Examples from Scotland reported to me by social workers include a young girl who was given DP under the guise of a glucose injection; and a short-stay patient in a mental hospital who was informed after having been given an injection that this was for contraception. (Mental patients are particularly vulnerable to this kind of abuse: it is, after all, almost as easy to give them the Pill without their knowledge, for they're often given six or seven pills a day anyway. Informed social workers suspect that DP as well as the Pill is not uncommonly given to unsuspecting women, e.g. to girls with little 'wrong' with them other than the label 'promiscuous'. In one working-class mental hospital in Scotland, it is fairly common knowledge among staff that DP is used in this way, 'especially by those psychiatrists who like zapping people with Modecate', as one of them put it to me. The case of a black 14-year-old from London serves as a final example of how DP can be given without the knowledge of the woman concerned: she had decided on the Pill, having changed her mind from the IUD, only to find that she had been given DP without her knowledge while she was under a general anaesthetic having an abortion. She only found out about this 'by accident' when she asked for her Pill prescription (case researched by Campaign Against Depo-Provera, 1979; see addresses at the end of this chapter).

I have already illustrated some of the factors at work which impinge on the question of choice for women in the Third World. The above example opens up the question of the vulnerability of their black sisters in the West. There are considerable grounds for the widespread belief that black and Asian women are being singled out in a racist way as prime targets for DP. Of those women who *are* asked for their consent, it is doubtful whether many of them are given even cursory details on which to base their decision.

Leeds is one of several places in Britain where DP is given to many Asian women at the same time as routine post-delivery rubella injections; examples have come to light of both black and white women – but mainly black – being told that they *must* have the DP injection with that for rubella (DP is never essential, and certainly not in these circumstances).[6] Furthermore, there are no grounds for the apparently prevalent belief that Asian women are more in need of rubella injections than their white sisters.[7]

Many health and social workers have expressed concern about what appears to be a racist approach to contraception among their colleagues, and the Campaign Against Depo-Provera is collecting information in this issue in an attempt to find out the extent of the problem.

There are many case histories of Asian women suffering side-effects from DP (such as uncontrollable bleeding) which they had not been warned about (and although an Urdu leaflet on DP was produced in Rochdale, a town with a high immigrant population, it omitted to discuss such problems as heavy bleeding).[8] In some cases doctors had not considered the symptoms important enough to warrant investigation, or had failed to grasp that symptoms such as dizziness, headaches, or even loss of periods, might in fact be side-effects of the drug. Sometimes, women had even been given another drug to counteract what their doctors had failed to recognise as side-effects from the first drug (personal communication; see also cases researched by the Campaign Against Depo-Provera).

Because DP does not require any action on the woman's part, some doctors seem to feel that they do not need to explain anything. Certainly, as a community health worker reports, they often find 'explaining' difficult, sometimes believing that 'these women' don't understand anything anyway. Another worker reports (Wilson, 1978):

> The women are treated not as human beings but as objects. Nurses and doctors point at them and talk about them as though they had no feelings. Their preferences are never sought. In addition there is the language problem . . . no hospital in this area employs interpreters.

Often women try to avoid going to the doctor or family planning clinic because the experience is so unpleasant. Their English teachers may sometimes accompany them, but, as one Leeds teacher illustrates, this is not necessarily much help:

> They treated N. very badly, like an idiot; never explained anything. The nurse constantly talked to me, not to N. She told me: 'These people have a low threshold of pain and can't be trusted to take pills regularly.'

> That's presumably why they got her on the injections. She's been on them for nearly three years now, with very bad headaches and back pain. She won't go to the clinic any more because they have been *so* unpleasant and rude, so she's stopped getting the injections.

Research by Wendy Savage (1978) suggests that large numbers of women in Britain, probably the vast majority, are inadequately informed about DP. Similarly, a study of 150 women interviewed by the US Institute for the Study of Medical Ethics reveals that few women had been warned of its possible dangers. With all this evidence, the following statement by the then Health Minister for England and Wales, Roland Moyle (1978), is interesting: 'I would expect a doctor prescribing any contraceptive to discuss fully with the patient the possible short- and long-term side effects.'

It would be misleading to leave the issue of consent without making clear the complexity of the subject in one important respect. Research has borne out that those in charge of giving out contraception largely dictate the contraceptives that women will 'choose', since their own prejudices govern the information put across as well as the contraceptives available (see, for example, Trussell *et al.*, 1976; Lane *et al.*, 1976). As Alan Guttmacher has pointed out (1970), 'It is my experience that the man [sic] in charge of the clinic largely dictates the contraceptive used in that clinic.' This phenomenon is by no means confined to the issue of DP, but it does contribute to our understanding of why those studies involving DP tend to report large numbers of women 'accepting' the drug, and puts in perspective the view that such studies involve giving 'balanced and unbiased information on a number of contraceptive methods including Depo-Provera' (Benagniano, 1978).

Much of the material on DP published by contraception 'experts' and bodies concerned with fertility regulation is unashamedly biased in favour of the drug. The IPPF (1978) describes DP and all injectable contraceptives as a 'most dependable and useful method of family planning, and that the IPPF system should continue to distribute them. . . . The alleged increased risk of carcinoma is not proven in the light of all the available evidence.' (Of course, as we shall see below, the 'alleged risk of carcinoma' is by no means *disproven*.) Malcolm Potts, doyen of the population control movement, comments (First Asian Regional Workshop, 1978; my emphasis):

> Other than a pregnant woman, any woman should be able to get Depo Provera from anyone who has a sharp needle and knows how to sterilize it. *We may need to modify this statement* with experience, but it represents a logical starting place for debate.

The remainder of this chapter examines the validity of such arguments. While doing so, however, it is important not to lose sight of the political bias of the population control movement described above.

The Medical Evidence

For reasons of space, the following is restricted to only some of the important aspects of DP. By concentrating on only a few of the important medical issues, I do not intend to imply that these are necessarily the most important, or the most controversial; DP's effect on breast-feeding, its effect on the cervix or on the lining of the womb are but three of the areas which should be considered in equal depth. Nevertheless, since so little information is normally available to women in the form of a serious critical evaluation of the evidence, a limited presentation of this sort is worthwhile, if only on the grounds that it may help readers as yet unconvinced of the need to question medical advice.

The reader may wish to keep two background factors in mind during the ensuing discussion. First, the standard 'three-monthly' dose of 150mg in fact lasts for more than three months (on average probably from 8-10 months according to Upjohn (1972a)). This is because the manufacturers need to cover themselves as far as effectiveness is concerned, so three months is less than the minimum period within which fertility has been demonstrated to return. Of course, this means that for those women who cannot tolerate the drug, side-effects will continue at least until it has been completely expelled from the body. Sometimes irregular and/or heavy bleeding (see below) can persist for a year or more after stopping the injection.

Secondly, we have to bear in mind serious deficiencies in the quality of much of the work on contraception – and much else to do with medical research. With studies concerning the safety of contraceptives, we have to bear in mind, for example, the numbers of women involved in the studies and the length of time they were on the drug, as well as the general research methods used. Taking just one of these factors, length of use, we find that research conclusions can be extremely misleading (see, for example, my analysis (Rakusen, 1974) of a much-quoted study of the Pill). With regard to DP, it can be equally difficult to work out the true significance of apparently impressive 'woman-years' of use, which in fact give no indication of the proportion of women on the drug for any given length of time. Thus, a study of, say, 1,000 woman-years could involve 500 women on DP for between 0 and 4 years, or any other combination involving the vast majority of women on short-term use. This deficiency inherent in many such studies renders them of doubtful meaning and liable to serious misapplication and misquotation.[9]

There are indeed few good studies anywhere involving DP. A number of experts told the US Select Committee that DP appeared to have fewer side effects than the Pill, and that there had never been any report of a death related to it, but as Deborah Maine (1978) points out, 'There are no studies of DP that are as well-designed and as carefully performed as those that document pill-associated mortality.' And as Dr Philip Corfman, director of the Center for Population Research, testified to the Select Committee (1978; my emphasis), 'We estimate that from three to five million women presently use this drug as a contraceptive worldwide, but unfortunately, *little effort has been made to follow these women to monitor long-term safety*.' It is worth bearing in mind that if one of the biggest DP studies did not involve giving women even cursory vaginal examinations for fear of putting them off (*People*, 1975a), it is doubtful whether it could shed any light on the suspicion that DP might increase the risk of cervical cancer. According to the Health Research Group (1976), Upjohn themselves compiled very little information on the women in their studies and provided no long-term follow-up. They submitted little information to the FDA on blood pressure changes in the women they studied, even though a significant number of such changes had been reported elsewhere (see Leiman, 1972).

Bearing in mind the overall inadequacy of much work in this area, we will now look at some aspects of DP in detail.

Bleeding problems

Most DP users experience bleeding problems (e.g. First Asian Regional Workshop, 1978). At first, they tend to involve frequent and/or heavy bleeding: 'As many as *11 to 30 days with bleeding per month* are seen in *10 to 35% of patients* in the first months of use' (Nash, 1975; my emphasis. See also Schwallie and Mohberg, 1977). The bleeding can stop quite soon, or continue for months. It can involve 'light spotting', or a constant, heavy flow; one woman's experience of the latter being, 'Really heavy bleeding: she never knew when she stood up whether she would end up with a spatter of blood at her feet.'

Apart from the inconvenience (at best) and total exhaustion and despair induced by such problems, they are also of concern physiologically. Anaemia could result, or be exacerbated, especially in undernourished women, and bleeding can mask serious problems as well as the (more rare) possibility of a hydatidiform mole.[10] To exclude such complications, women often need to undergo a dilation and curettage (D and C), an operation to explore the inside of the uterus which itself is not without risk, especially for post-partum (recently-delivered) mothers.

DP after childbirth

Several people have expressed concern to me about DP's role in post-partum bleeding. One GP working in east London is finding large numbers of women put on DP before being discharged from hospital into her care; another speaks of the numbers of mostly Asian women that she saw at University College Hospital, London, who were still bleeding a lot at six weeks post-partum (when bleeding should in fact have stopped). She felt the bleeding was most unlikely to have been caused by anything other than DP. Now working as a GP, she is seeing another woman who is still bleeding six months after her baby was born, having had only one injection of DP. Despite the problems that DP can cause for post-partum women[11] – women who are in any case often in an extremely vulnerable state – it appears that increasing numbers of women are being injected with DP at this time.

Experience at the London Hospital (Savage, 1978) showed that a considerable proportion of women with heavy bleeding underwent D and Cs, which the author rightly refers to as iatrogenically induced (i.e. medically induced, in that the women concerned had been given an inappropriate drug – DP). Some doctors believe that diagnostic D and Cs are only rarely necessary and that oestrogens can be used instead (see below). However, even Upjohn themselves say (1972b) that the possibility should be borne in mind that a D and C may be necessary – 'if only to be sure that some underlying condition . . . may not be responsible' – and it is the D and C that is the more likely to exclude such underlying and potentially dangerous conditions.

Added oestrogen

In spite of the fact that oestrogen is not always useful in 'controlling' bleeding (see, for example, El Habashy *et al.*, 1970), many practitioners advocate its use for that purpose (First Asian Workshop, 1978). Some use it routinely with DP (See, for example, McDaniel and Pardthaisong, 1974), and some though not all of them give oestrogen throughout the cycle (see, for example, Dodds, 1971). McDaniel (1973) reports that 'one world-recognised authority in Chile estimates that approximately 40% of his patients eventually require an oral oestrogen supplement'.

Whatever the regimes given, the use of DP becomes increasingly questionable when another potent drug with its own potential side-effects is used to combat those of the first drug, particularly when (a) the woman concerned had no need of drug treatment in the first place; and (b) the promoters of the first drug – DP – argue that it is valuable precisely because it is not considered to be implicated with the same risks as oral contraceptives containing oestrogen. The American FDA did not fail to grasp this point when it decided, in part for this reason, to refuse the manufacturers a general licence for DP (Finkel, 1978; Finkel was Associate Director for New Drug Evaluation, FDA).

Absent periods

After the first year or so on DP, complete absence of bleeding (amenorrhoea) becomes a problem. This in turn raises another problem: diagnosis of any pregnancy becomes very difficult. As with the Pill, a woman can go several months before she realises she is pregnant; if she doesn't want the baby, she may well find getting an abortion impossible at this stage, and if she wants to keep it she has to face the unknown possibility of a malformed baby, as well as difficulty in pin-pointing the foetus's length of gestation.

The medical implications of long-term, DP-induced amenorrhoea seem to have been somewhat neglected in the medical literature. I have, however, found mention of this issue in the evidence of Toppozada (1978) given to the US Select Committee, who testified as follows:

> Very little is known about the possible risks induced by cycle alterations caused by Depo Provera . . . the impact of prolonged amenorrhoea upon the health of users is poorly understood. What would the cycle alterations impose upon the state of health among women with endemic diseases or with metabolic disorders is another unresolved question. . . . There is a paucity of information regarding any metabolic disturbances or hormonal changes related to prolonged amenorrhoea.

The rest of the time, the medical establishment seems to

regard amenorrhoea purely as a socio-cultural problem – that for 'irrational' reasons, women do not like their periods to cease. So, at the First Asian Regional Workshop (1978), for example, it is reported that amenorrhoea is 'treated by most clinicians with reassurance, and education that this status in *not harmful*' (my italics); some programmes are reported to 'emphasise the beneficial aspects of amenorrhoea'. There are many such complacent reports that women have 'irrational' fears of blood building up in their wombs and causing headaches and cancer (see, for example, Seitz, 1979). One has only to read Ehrenreich and English (1979), a book documenting countless medical myths about women, to see where women's 'irrational' fears come from.

Medical attitudes to the Pill indicate a similar lack of concern: it is now fashionable among some proponents of population control to advocate taking the Pill without a break, so that no regular bleeding is induced, yet at the same time, sparse discussion takes place on the possible harm of this regimen. There are, however, few grounds for the belief that monthly, pill-induced bleeding is necessarily any better!

Infertility

Allied to bleeding problems, particularly amenorrhoea, are doubts concerning the return of fertility following the cessation of DP injections. Many doctors claim these fears are groundless (see, for example, First Asian Regional Workshop, 1978).

There is insufficient evidence for such claims as no study has yet been completed that is either adequately designed or has run sufficiently long for this question to be answered. Nash (1975), for example, states that although the data (to his mind) are sufficiently extensive to guarantee that most women regain their fertility after stopping DP, 'They are not sufficiently extensive to assure that normal fertility rates return.' Three years later, Prof. Allan Rosenfield clearly felt the same way, informing the US Select Committee hearings that women should be warned about the possible delayed return of fertility and, in some cases, about the potential for absence of return of fertility. Benagniano (1976) repeated the World Health Organization's recommendations of the previous year that, until there was conclusive evidence concerning the return of fertility, users should be warned that future fertility may be impaired. Vecchio, head of medical research at Upjohn, himself says (Vecchio, 1974) that 'it is . . . indeed likely that some cases will be found of "over-suppression", that is, failure of normal endogenous hormonal mechanisms to become reactivated after the disappearance of the drug effect', and one significant finding (Scutchfield *et al.*, 1971) is that the more prolonged the use of DP, the slower the return of menstruation (and presumably, therefore, of ovulation).

Needless to say, many programmes involving DP do not involve women who have had no children, young women (say under 30), or women who have not completed their families (e.g. Apelo *et al.*, 1974; Azcona, 1977). At Chieng Mai in Thailand, which has one of the biggest projects on DP – and which is widely quoted as showing that subsequent fertility rates are not impaired – many women who have not had a child, and therefore demonstrated that they are fertile, were excluded from the DP study. The reason given for excluding such women was that unknowingly infertile women would tend to blame their infertility on the doctors prescribing DP, and on the drug itself (McDaniel, 1973). The exclusion of so many categories of women from much research on DP is another reason for regarding blanket statements about the drug's innocuous effect on subsequent fertility as highly questionable. Furthermore, large numbers of women at Chieng Mai have also been given oestrogen supplements routinely (e.g. see McDaniel and Pardthaisong, 1974) and, as Nash (1975) points out, 'This may have prevented the endometrium [lining of the womb] from becoming as atrophic as it might with DP alone.'

Thus, there are many reasons to be cautious of any sweeping claims concerning impressive long-term and conclusive studies. So far, we can be sure that DP delays the return of fertility, on average for three months longer than the Pill. But this knowledge may well be relevant only for women given DP well after their periods had become established, and women of proven fertility.

It is worthwhile to recall here that even after many more years of study on the effects of the contraceptive pill, its effect on possible permanent damage to fertility in some users is not clear.

Other side-effects

Many other side-effects are associated with DP, as with the Pill, and their reported incidence varies from study to study. Nash (1975), for instance, cites headache, abdominal discomfort, nervousness, dizziness, decreased libido, asthma, limb pain, nausea, breast discomfort, peripheral oedema, backache, depression, fatigue, and diarrhoea – all of them, incidentally under the heading 'subjective' side-effects (the term 'subjective' could perhaps be applied with more reason to the author of that particular review).

The relationship between such symptoms and DP has received scant attention. However, examination of a study of progestogen-only pills suggests to me that similar mechanisms may be operating with DP – which is also, of course, a product which contains solely a progestogen. This well-designed study (Vessey *et al.*, 1972) looked at four groups of women, each on a different progestogen-only pill, and a fifth 'control' group on a 'combination' pill. Pain in the back or abdomen – a problem experienced by some women on DP – was the principal problem noted by progestogen-only pill users (although 60-70 per cent were reportedly entirely free from side-effects unrelated to menstrual disturbances). The women on the combination pill experienced nausea and vomiting to a greater extent than the others, but a considerable number of the latter had headaches, the incidence rate being higher with all the progestogen-only pills than with the combination pill.[12] Other side-effects experienced by some of the progestogen-only pill users included: irritability, vertigo, aggravation of varicose veins, reduced libido, unusual fatigue, thinning of the hair, aggravation of asthma, unusual thirst, vaginal itching and, again, diarrhoea. 'Most of them', say Vessey *et al.*, 'have been reported as side effects of progestogen-only contraceptives in other trials and therefore deserve mention here.' Significantly, two of the pills in this trial contained chlormadinone acetate and megestrol acetate which, as mentioned earlier, are very closely related to the progestogen in DP.

Participants in the First Asian Regional Workshop found that with DP, dizziness was the most common non-menstrual complaint, at least in two projects carried out in the Third World; in Hong Kong, however, this side-effect was apparently rare. The discrepancy in reported incidence of dizziness, far from leading to the problem being regarded as culturally induced or dismissed in some other way, led participants to postulate that nutrition may play a part in the cause of the symptoms, as well as low blood pressure.

Loss of libido is a side-effect commonly dismissed with 'reassurance'. But Upjohn themselves (Vecchio, 1972) list decreased libido as a possible side effect of DP, and theoretically there are indeed reasons for this: progestogen is known to suppress sexual activity in non-human mammals, for example, and it has been suggested that the progestogen in the Pill might play a part in suppressing the mid-cycle peak in women's sexual interest that seems to occur with the Pill (Adams *et al.*, 1978).

Some researchers (e.g. Wilson, 1976) report that few women drop out of their studies because of side-effects. Wilson suggests that perhaps her low drop-out rate could be due to the 'personal care and support' given, and the careful explanation of menstrual irregularities. Personal care, support, and reassurance, even concerning apparently non-life-threatening side-effects, is only caring, supportive, or reassuring if it is based on sound evidence. Commonly, this evidence is lacking.

Research on breast cancer

Treatment of the breast cancer issue is one of several disturbing examples of the way in which research conclusions are distorted and biased in favour of DP.

We have already seen how, although the injectable form of DP is widely available, oral contraceptives containing DP and its related compounds have been withdrawn from the market because they were all shown to induce breast tumours in beagles. As well as ignoring this blatant inconsistency, advocates of DP take great care to question the validity of those very 'Wretched Beagle' studies (to quote Upjohn, 1973). Broadly, they argue that: (1) the studies are of no relevance to humans since the affected dogs were 'given enormous doses of Depo-Provera, not comparable to those used in humans' (McDaniel, 1978); and (2) that beagles are an inappropriate comparison.

The first point is a little surprising since Upjohn themselves reveal (1973) that, although in one study four dogs were given only low doses of DP, *three* of them developed persistent breast nodules. Of these four dogs, two died within three years; while of those dogs used as 'controls' (i.e. they were given no drug at all), *none* died spontaneously (two were, however, killed for research purposes and found to be normal, and a third died 'in a fight').

The argument that beagles are an inappropriate species for comparison with humans is put forward vociferously by many interested parties although, as the US public interest Health Research Group points out (1976), if no problems were shown up in these beagle studies, few would be arguing that the animals used were inappropriate. It is, in fact, to some extent true that the beagles were an inappropriate animal from which to draw unequivocal conclusions, for they are known to be susceptible to certain progestogens and to breast nodules in general (IARC, 1974). (However, since animal studies are notoriously difficult to interpret, few would feel able to draw unequivocal conclusions with regard to most animal studies.)[13] It can also be argued that beagles should be used precisely because they are sensitive to progestogens. And even if dogs do metabolise DP differently from humans, there is no scientific basis for dismissing the evidence as irrelevant to humans – as, for example, McDaniel (1978) does – if DP itself, as opposed to its metabolites, is the cancer-inducing agent.[14] No one has yet shown what the possible cancer-inducing agent is. Finally, the 'control' dogs did not have a high incidence of tumours and, in fact, showed a 'remarkably low incidence' as pointed out by two industry scientists quoted by the Health Research Group (1976).

Much of the research on this and related issues is not publicly available for scrutiny (it is a problem common to all drug research that there seems to be no way in which manufacturers can be obliged to publish their work so that people independent of commercial and other vested interests can review it). However, even Upjohn conclude (1973), in a paper which attempts to discount the beagle studies, that more work is necessary 'to rule out an effect on the breast in the human'.

In conclusion, it must be remembered that, although by itself the evidence on beagles is equivocal, similar evidence led to the withdrawal of similar progestogens. More recently, the Department of Health and Social Security ordered the withdrawal of the antihistamine drug, methapyrilene, on the basis of liver tumours found in rats (they were given the drug continuously over their life-span at 25-30 times the human dose). It issued a press statement (DHSS, 1979; my italics) which is interesting when looked at in the context of the foregoing discussion: '*While there is no evidence that a similar effect would occur in human beings* it is considered that *any possibility of potential carcinogenic risk* to man (sic) is *sufficient to justify the action taken*'. There are at least three reasons why DP should be regarded with, if anything, more caution than methapyrilene: it is primarily used as a contraceptive and as such is intended for healthy women and not for ill people; and it has far more potential for both long-term and continuous use.

In the light of the above discussion, the beagle studies can hardly be dismissed, whatever their shortcomings.

Research performed on *women* is also used to argue that we have nothing to fear, and the 'fact' that DP does not cause breast tumours in women is constantly repeated by DP promoters. Another way of presenting information on this aspect of DP is to say that the research to date cannot provide us with the necessary information – a slightly different version of the truth. Two of the few published studies on the subject of DP's effect on women's breasts will be considered below.

Zanartu *et al.* (1973) embarked on their study in 1963-4. They disarmingly report: 'Fertile young women exposed to almost constant progestational effect have been studied in a prospective design in search of eventual iatrogenicity [in other words, medically-induced disease] for the human breast.' This study was, incidentally, on poor women in Latin America. No controls were used, so the data are difficult to interpret, but although the incidence of tumours is small, it has an interesting distribution: of the 330 women who had used DP for five years or more, two – aged 23 and 33 (i.e. in an age-range where the incidence would be expected to be one of the lowest) – developed breast cancer. The results of this study are rarely commented upon in this way, but rather in the context of 3,350 women having been given DP, out of whom 'only two' got breast cancer. (An exception to this is an editorial comment on this paper in the 1974 Obstetrical and Gynaecological Survey which comments that the beagle data might well be relevant to humans on the basis that the two cancers found were in young women who had used the drug for a relatively long time.)

One project commonly referred to as showing that DP does not cause breast lumps in women is that based at Chieng Mai (see McDaniel and Pardthaisong, 1973; McDaniel, 1973; Pardthaisong *et al.*, 1975). However, women had been followed up at most for about eight years, and many of them used the drug only for a relatively short period (Pardthaisong *et al.* (1975) report that only 45 per cent of the women used DP for as long as three years). In addition, supplementary oestrogens were given routinely to many of the women, at least until comparatively recently (and on this point it has been postulated that continuous progestogen given without oestrogen is more likely to encourage cancer growth than if given together with it (Rinehart and Winter, 1975)).

Notwithstanding all this, the Chieng Mai researchers found not totally dissimilar results from Zanartu: although they report finding no cases of cancer and only eight women reporting breast nodules out of 1,527 women, 503 of the women had received only four injections or less (i.e. had received DP for less than two years); of the eight women with nodules, five had received eighteen injections or more. No one knows if the development of these types of nodules predisposes women to getting breast cancer, but three of the five were reported to have no symptoms at a subsequent examination.

The widely reported observation that DP appears to increase milk production in some breast-feeding women is also relevant to the breast cancer issue for, as the Health Research Group (1976) points out, 'This increase indicates that DP may have a constant stimulatory effect on the production of the hormone prolactin' (a condition that may be related to breast cancer).

No study to date has unequivocally shown that DP is related to breast cancer in humans. Nor has anyone shown the opposite to be the case. Much of the research has been equivocal or inadequate, and none of it has been conducted for long enough. As Nash (1975) stresses, 'The need for studies of long duration is indicated by the fact that the incidence of nodules in dogs did not increase markedly until after three years.' In the meantime, suggestive evidence, especially when taken all together, gives cause for concern. Whether any properly informed woman would willingly take part in such long-term trials is another question.

Discussion

It is evident that the range of contraceptive choices open to women is very much governed by commercial and/or population control interests, together with the prejudices and competence of their doctors. With regard to DP, the information that a woman receives tends to come from sources which are weighted in favour of the drug, and even apparently independent advisers such as GPs themselves obtain their information for the most part from such sources (directly or indirectly). It is in this light that any professed commitment of organisations like the IPPF to a woman's right to choose should be seen. (For example, Julia Henderson, then president of the IPPF, wrote to the *Guardian* (1977) in response to an article questioning the use of DP, saying that her organisation 'considers that women have the right to make their own choice among the approved methods . . . .')

In this final section I want to discuss in a slightly broader context (1) research and information relating to DP; and (2) the question of DP's dangers in relation to birth control as a whole, and the appropriate feminist response.

Research and the feminist demand for full information

In the foregoing discussion, I have touched on some of the drawbacks and difficulties in evaluating much research on DP and contraception as a whole. The feminist demand for access to 'full information' thus becomes extremely complex, and it is doubtful that we can *begin* to be properly informed unless feminist ideology permeates the information process. But in addition, access to information is of limited value without the ability to understand and evaluate it. One of the dangerous positions into which women are being increasingly pushed is that, while being given some information (for instance the latest package inserts for the Pill), most of us are totally ill-equipped to evaluate and use it. While working on the feminist demand for 'full information', we need also to work towards creating a climate where people *feel* in charge of their own bodies; where people can expect to be conversant with the fundamentals of statistics (which is a means by which many of us are manipulated and mystified in all aspects of our lives), and with the sciences concerned with the human body. We need to cultivate a healthy disrespect for 'experts' in any field, to learn to question and to doubt. Doctors' roles as experts, even in areas outside their expertise, have gone unquestioned for a long time, and it requires a lot of consciousness-raising and commitment on our part to learn to use them solely as advisers and technicians.

At the same time, it would be easy – and wrong – to leave the issues of research and information as problems associated with the fact that our researchers and informers are biased. Alongside political considerations, we must take into account the quality of medical research, and that of evaluative thinking in general. To put it in terms of 'us and them': although we would be wise to start with the assumption that all information emanating from 'them' is suspect, we cannot assume that the information produced by 'us' (here I am referring to feminists, like myself, and their supporters) is beyond dispute and good. An article in the *British Medical Journal* (Gore *et al.*, 1977), concerned with evaluating a sample of published articles in the same journal, found that 32 had statistical errors of various kinds, 18 being 'fairly serious faults', and in *at least* 5 of them, conclusions were drawn which were 'unsupportable on re-examination of the data'.

This illustrates the need for critically reviewing medical research before using it. Needless to say, in my own efforts, I am often struck by the great difficulty I sometimes have of critically reviewing material that fits in with my own preconceptions! However, I am sometimes amazed at the limited understanding that is apparently considered sufficient by some publications that espouse, or are sympathetic to, the feminist cause. In the case of DP, for example, references have been made to its being an 'extremely dangerous drug' (by implication more so than, say, the Pill), as having a 'distinctly nasty effect on the patient' (and by implication all women), and as not licensed for general use 'mainly due to the risk of breast and cervical cancer' (thereby implying that there was a distinct, proven risk). All these statements muddy the facts and limit our political understanding of the issues involved. The need to be rigorous in evaluating and presenting information is thus an important – and neglected – area of feminist (and socialist) thinking.

The relative dangers of DP: what do we do?

Toxicity with sex steroid hormones such as oestrogens and progestogens is a very complicated subject and the issues are not clear-cut. For example, as a (feminist) researcher in this area explained to me, one would expect such hormones to cause cancer or even kill if given in very large doses, precisely because they stimulate growth, but that does not necessarily mean that low doses of such drugs would have the same effect.

In one sense, that makes the beagle studies explored above even more equivocal, although of course dogs given DP at low doses did also develop (non-malignant) tumours. But they also appear more equivocal in another sense, for there is more published evidence that the synthetic oestrogens contained in the Pill, and even some of the natural oestrogens that we produce in our own bodies, given in large doses are carcinogenic: cancerous tumours have been induced in more sites and in less 'controversial' animals than with DP (International Agency for Research on Cancer, 1974; Committee on Safety of Medicines, 1972).

It is not possible in this space to make a detailed comparison of the dangers of different contraceptives. However, in many respects we just don't know enough about any of them (see, for example, Kellhammer and Uberla, 1977), and a good case could be made for actually banning the Pill and the IUD, on the grounds of deaths and disease caused by both. While DP is suspect with regard to causing infertility, so is the Pill, but the IUD is *known* to cause infertility in a percentage of users who develop pelvic inflammatory disease because of infections, and women in areas where gonorrhoea is rife, especially in the Third World, are particularly at risk from this.

Thus, to single out DP as dangerous can lead to confusion. It tends to result in DP being labelled the arch-villain, eclipsing the known and as yet unknown dangers of other methods, including female sterilisation, while at the same time the problems of who controls research, promotion, and information, etc. remain. Focusing solely on the drawbacks of DP can lull women into a false sense of security about the other, non-barrier methods of contraception.

On present knowledge, the case for banning DP lies more with the fact that it is one of the methods least in control of the woman herself, and the way it is used. However, were the feminist movement to succeed in obtaining a ban on the drug, there would be many other injectable contraceptives which could take its place (e.g. see Benagniano, 1976). Noristerat, which is close to being the second choice after DP, is already thought to produce tumours in the pituitary and mammary glands of rats (but apparently not in beagles!). And unless the ban applied worldwide, the drug would be dumped in Third World countries where women are least able to resist its use. Finally, the possible ban of DP should not blind us to the fact that abuses with other methods of contraception have occurred, and will continue to do so unless far-reaching changes take place.[15]

One of the changes necessary is for abortion to become a right for all women. Abortion is inextricably bound up with the DP issue – as it is with the contraception issue as a whole. Unless abortion is freely available, many women will always feel fearful enough of unwanted pregnancies to 'choose' the more effective – even if less safe – methods of contraception, doctors will tend to slant their advice in favour of these 'effective' methods, and to administer them sometimes without the proper consent of the woman involved, and drug companies and population control agencies will continue to ply their worldwide trade with these methods to the exclusion of others.

It is said by the proponents of DP that women actually beg for it, sometimes travelling many miles over rough country to get it (see, for example, *People* 1975b; Wilson 1979).[16] The implication is that DP must be good if women act in this way. But what is open to question is (a) whether such women are adequately informed about the drug; (b) whether there are in fact viable alternatives open to them; and of course (c) whether those dispensing DP in these circumstances aren't themselves biasing their advice in favour of it. Significantly, among those women reported to be happy on DP are those whose husbands refuse to allow them to use contraceptives; this is the case particularly with some Roman Catholic and Asian families. Men have been known to throw pills away, forcibly to remove IUDs, and beat their wives for using contraception, and it is understandable that women faced with this kind of problem might welcome an injectable contraceptive. DP, in these circumstances, could seem the least oppressive alternative to the women concerned, although of course it does nothing to change their basic situation and can even be used to maintain the *status quo*. But the banning of DP could be seen by such women to be yet another oppressive cross to bear.

The question of whether or not DP should be banned is, therefore, a problematic one. Aiming to do so can hardly be seen as a serious infringement of a woman's right to choose for, as I have shown, most women have few rights in the matter of choosing contraception anyway. However, I am unconvinced that this is the right course of action, particularly if it is taken on its own. My doubts centre on the unavoidable implication that the other non-barrier methods are less damaging. Other doubts include the fact that the drug would have to be totally withdrawn if the ban were to be effective, otherwise the situation would be no different than already exists, at least in Britain: here, for example, although the drug is only licensed for short-term use in very limited circumstances, the fact that it is available at all enables doctors to use their 'clinical judgment' to prescribe the drug in whatever way they like. The total withdrawal of DP would mean withholding its availability for treating some conditions for which it is regarded as effective – and also, incidentally, for some conditions for which it is widely used despite the fact that it is completely ineffective.

In Britain, the Campaign Against Depo-Provera has two other aims in addition to the withdrawal of the drug: to expose the way in which it has been developed, experimented and used on women; and 'free, safe and reliable contraception on demand'. As a single-issue campaign, it is inevitable that the attack should focus on DP to the relative neglect of *all* contraceptives used in an exploitative, dangerous and ill-informed way. However, feminists need to be equally concerned about the uncontrolled distribution of the Pill and IUD, for example, especially in the Third World, and about the inadequate information women tend to receive with regard to all methods (one has only to look at current leaflets provided for women in British birth control clinics to question the quality of information available). If DP were ever to be withdrawn, together with all other injectable contraceptives, it is not unlikely, at least in the short term, that the IUD would replace them, leading, incidentally, to more cases of women with iatrogenically-induced infertility than would DP, on the basis of our present knowledge (or lack of it).

In this chapter I have looked at some of the issues raised by DP[17], and indicated, I hope, how other methods of contraception raise similar crucial issues. Whatever our short-term aims with regard to DP, women need to question the adequacy of all contraceptive research programmes, of all medical follow-up, and of all systemic birth control methods. The need for redirecting all contraceptive research (to borrow the title of Judy Norsigian's important paper (1979)) remains, as does the need for assessing the kind of, and quality of, research that we are prepared to accept. How many of us, for instance, would knowingly and willingly act as guinea pigs in programmes involving any form of systemic contraception? Yet that is what millions of women are currently doing: with DP, with the IUD, and with the Pill. How many women would act as the very same guinea pigs if they knew that the research projects were failing in the most fundamental ways to ask the right questions, and to do even minimal follow-up? Finally, to return to the abortion issue: if early abortion were freely available, how many women would feel the need to put their bodies and lives at risk with *any* systemic or invasive methods of contraception?

Addresses

Campaign Against Depo-Provera, c/o ICAR, 374 Gray's Inn Road, London WC1.
International Campaign for Abortion Rights, 374 Gray's Inn Road, London WC1.
National Abortion Campaign, 374 Gray's Inn Road, London WC1.
Pill Victims' Action Group, c/o Ms Judith Challenger, 3 Eney Close, Abingdon, Oxon.
Women's Research and Resources Centre, 190 Upper Street, London N1.

Notes

1 The UK Committee on Safety of Medicines has also come under repeated pressure to lift its licensing restrictions on the drug; indeed by the time you read this, it may well have done just that.

However, whatever the CSM may say, and whatever licences it sanctions, doctors' 'clinical freedom' allows them to prescribe how they like unless the relevant drug is completely withdrawn from the market. It is widely acknowledged that DP is commonly prescribed in circumstances which do not fulfil the CSM's criteria.

2 For more details about the FDA's attitude, see Deborah Maine (1978).

3 If the tenuous evidence mentioned in this report is confirmed, other progestogens will be implicated, as well as the progestogen contained in DP; the links between these rare and dangerous liver tumours and the contraceptive pill (which contains a combination of an oestrogen and a progestogen) are already established.

4 From a telephone conversation with an IPPF doctor.

5 The domination of Western capitalist interests over Third World population control programmes has been well documented elsewhere (e.g. Mamdami, 1973; Mass, 1976; George, 1976).

6 Reports include evidence collected by the National Childbirth Trust, community workers, and English Language teachers; some women have even been refused rubella injections unless they agreed to an injection of DP as well.

7 Telephone conversation with Dr Bill Marshall, Dept Infectious Diseases, Great Ormond Street Hospital for Sick Children, London.

8 Heavy and unpredictable bleeding patterns are particularly problematic for Muslim and certain other orthodox women.

9 In addition, many of the secondary sources which doctors read and use fail to recognise the problem, talking of thousands of women-years of use as 'evidence' of the harmlessness of a drug (with regard to DP, see for example, Azcona, 1977; McDaniel, 1978; Smith, 1978). I have even seen, as we go to press, one medical magazine referring to 'published information covering 275,000 woman *months'* (my emphasis) as 'clinical evidence' of the drug's safety.

10 A complication of pregnancy where the placenta becomes abnormally large and the embryo fails to develop, the uterus becoming full of fluid-filled cells.

11 As mentioned above, these problems also extend to difficulties with lactation, and to the unknown effects of relatively large quantities of DP ingested by the baby.

12 Vecchio (1973), Upjohn's head of research, asserts that although there are frequent reports of headaches in women given DP for contraceptive purposes, headache is not reported in women receiving 80 times this dose for the treatment of endometrial cancer, which, he says, 'makes one doubt that headache is a drug-related occurrence'. He does not discuss any of the work relating to the progestogen-only pill and does not explain how knowledge concerning users suffering from cancer was accumulated. Nor do we at any point encounter a consideration of what perhaps is causing the headaches, a similar situation to that seen with the Pill.

13 The value and meaning of animal studies is an extremely complex area – about which most clinicians know very little. For further reading on the value – or lack of it – of many kinds of animal studies, see Richard Peto in 'Long Term Hazards from Environmental Chemicals' (papers from a Royal Society discussion meeting, December 1977, published by the Royal Society in 1979).

14 DP is converted in the body to other chemical substances ('metabolites') before these are removed from the body via the urine.

15 I have already mentioned sterilisation abuses. Recent examples include a Sri Lankan woman being told that she would not be given milk powder unless she were sterilised or had an IUD inserted (*People*, vol. 5, issue 2, 1978, p. 8), and in the *Guardian* for 3 July 1979, Angela Phillips and Jill Nicholls report three different stories of women who, after one abortion at an early stage of pregnancy, were pushed reluctantly, or against their will, into using injectable contraceptives, the Pill or an IUD – all of which, of course, carry health risks.

16 Elizabeth Wilson is a family planning doctor in Glasgow.

17 Obviously, with medical evidence, new information is emerging all the time. However, at the time of going to press, the information I have collected since writing this chapter does not fundamentally affect the points raised.

References

Adams, D. B., Ross Gold, A., Burt, A.D. (1978), 'Rise in female-initiated sexual activity at ovulation and its suppression by oral contraceptives', *New England Journal of Medicine*, vol. 229, no. 21, 11 November, pp. 1145-50.

Apelo, R.A., de la Cruz, J.R., Lopez, F.C. (1974), 'Acceptability of injectable contraception in the Philippines', *IPPF Medical Bulletin*, vol. 8, no. 2, pp. 1-2.

Azcona, S.C. (1977), 'Three monthly Depo-Provera in Mexico', *IPPS Medical Bulletin*, vol. 11, no. 3.

Benagniano, G. (1976), 'Long-acting systemic contraceptives', in WHO Symposium on Advances in Fertility Regulation, held in Moscow, pp. 323-60.

Benagniano, G. (1978), statement made by Benagniano, of the World Health Organization, to the US Select Committee Hearings on Population, US House of Representatives, held August 1978. Taken from summary of the transcripts, produced by Program for the Introduction and Adaptation of Contraceptive Technology, and available on file at Women's Research and Resources Centre, London, or direct from PIACT, 4000 N.E. 41st St. (PO Box C-5395), Seattle, Washington 98105, USA.

Boston Women's Health Package (1978), letter dated September, on file at Women's Research and Resources Centre, London.

Business Week (1979), 'The labs' search for safer birth control', quoting Dr S.D. Matunda, 16 April.

Committee on Safety of Medicines (1972), *Carcinogenicity Tests of Oral Contraceptives*, HMSO, London.

Corea, G. (1978), open letter to the American Food and Drug Administration, September; circulated in Boston Women's Health Package and available from Women's Research and Resources Centre, London.

Corfman, P.A. (1978), evidence to US Select Committee Hearings on Population, US House of Representatives (see Benagniano, 1978, for details).

Department of Health and Social Security (1979), 'Anti-histamine drug to be withdrawn', press statement on methapyrilene issued 6 July.

Dodds, G.H. (1971), 'Depo Provera', in *Proceedings of 5th Asian Congress of Obstetrics and Gynaecology*, pp. 169-75, Djakarta.

Ehrenreich, B., and English, D. (1979), *For Her Own Good: 150 Years of the Experts' Advice to Women*, Pluto Press, London.

El Habashy, M.A., Mishell, D.R., Moyer, D.L. (1970), 'Effect of supplementary oral oestrogen on long-acting injectable progestogen contraception', *Obstetrics and Gynaecology*, vol. 35, pp. 51-4.

Family Planning Perspectives (1979), 'DP may be linked to Uterine Cancer, Preliminary Data Imply', vol. 11, issue 1, p. 47.

Finkel, M. (1978), Associate Director for New Drug Evaluation, FDA, letter to Upjohn, 7 March, quoted by PIACT (see Benagniano, 1978, for details).

First Asian Regional Workshop on Injectable Contraceptives (1978), May, Thailand, on file at IPPF library, or available from McCormick Hospital (see McDaniel, 1973).

George, S. (1976), *How the Other Half Dies*, Penguin, London.

Girotti and Hauser (1970), *Therapeutische Umschau und medizinische Bibliographie*, Band 27, p. 671, Bern.

Gore, S.M. *et al* (1977), 'Misuse of statistical methods: critical assessment of articles in BMJ from January to March 1976', *British Medical Journal*, 8 January.

Guttmacher, A. (1970), Evidence to US Senate Pill Committee Hearings. Hearings before the sub-committee on Monopoly of the Select Committee on Small Business, US Senate, 2nd session on present status of competition in the pharmaceutical industry, Parts 15, 16 and 17; *Oral Contraceptives*, vols 1, 2 and 3. Hearings held from January to March 1970.

Health Research Group (1976), 'Depo-Provera – a contraceptive for poor women', public letter to Theodore Cooper, Assistant Secretary for Health at US Dept of Health, Education and Welfare, December. On file at Women's Research and Resources Centre, London.

Henderson, J. (1977), letter to London *Guardian*, 7 July.

International Agency for Research on Cancer (1974), monograph on the evaluation of carcinogenic risk of chemicals to man (*sic*), *Sex Hormones*, vol. 6, Lyon.

International Planned Parenthood Federation (1978), *Factsheets* on Depo-Provera, available from IPPF.

Kader, M.M., Aziz, M.T. Abdel, Bahgat, M.R., Kamal, I., Talat, M., Abdallah, Osman, M. (1975), 'Effect of two long acting injectable progestogens on lactation in the human', *Acta Biologica et Medica Germanica*, Band 34, pp. 1199-204, Berlin.

Kellhammer and Uberla (eds) (1977), 'Long-term studies on side effects of contraception – state and planning', *Lecture Notes on Medical Informatics*, vol. 3, Springer-Verlag, Munich.

Lane, M.E., Arceo, R., Sobrero, A.J. (1976), 'Successful use of the diaphragm and jelly', *Family Planning Perspectives*, vol. 8, no. 2, pp. 81-6.

Leiman, G. (1972), 'Depo medroxyprogesterone acetate as a contraceptive agent: its effect on weight and blood pressure', *American Journal of Obstetrics and Gynaecology*, 1 September, vol. 114, no. 1, pp. 97-102.

McDaniel, E.B. (1973), 'Mini-manual for use of DMPA', unpublished. Available from Dr McDaniel at McCormick Hospital, Box 56, Chieng Mai, Thailand.

McDaniel, E.B. (1978), 'More on Injectables', letter to *People*, vol. 5, issue 1.

McDaniel, E.B., and Pardthaisong, T. (1973), 'Incidence of breast nodules in women receiving multiple doses of medroxyprogesterone acetate', *Journal of Biosocial Science*, vol. 5, pp. 83-8.

McDaniel, E.B., and Pardthaisong, T. (1974), 'Use Effectiveness of six-month injections of DMPA as a contraceptive', *American Journal of Obstetrics and Gynaecology*, 15 May, vol. 119, no. 2.

Maine, D. (1978), 'Depo – the debate continues', *Family Planning Perspectives*, vol. 10, no. 6, pp. 342-5.

Mamdami, M. (1973), *The Myth of Population Control*, Monthly Review Press, New York and London.

Mass, B. (1976), *Population Target – the political economy of Population Control in Latin America*, Latin American Working Group, Canada.

Minkin, S. (1979), 'Aid Pills Harm Women and Children', mimeographed paper on file at Women's Research and Resources Centre.

Moyle, R. (1978), in response to a Parliamentary Question from John Tilley, MP, asking whether he was satisfied that all women were warned about the short-term and long-term possible side effects; December, Hansard vol. 964, col. 576-7; written answer dated 20 March.

Nash, H.A. (1975), 'Depo Provera – a Review', *Contraception*, vol. 12, no. 4, pp. 377-93.

Nissen, E.D., Kent, D.R., Nissen, S.E. (1976), 'Liver tumors and the Pill: analyzing the data', *Contemporary Ob/Gyn*, November, vol. 8, pp. 103-11.

Norsigian, J. (1979), 'Redirecting Contraceptive Research', testimony presented on behalf of the US National Women's Health Network at the US Select Committee on Population, House of Representatives, 1978, and subsequently published in *Science for People*, January/February 1979, pp. 27-30.

Obstetrical and Gynaecological Survey (1974), 'Mammary Gland Nodules in Women under Continuous Exposure to Progestogens', vol. 29, pp. 83-4.

Pardthaisong, T., McDaniel, E.B., Gray, R.H. (1975), 'Acceptance and use of Depo Provera in Chieng Mai', *IPPF Medical Bulletin*, vol. 9, issue 1.

Parveen, L., Chowdhury, A.Q., Chowdhury, Z. (1977), 'Injectable contraception (medroxyprogesterone acetate) in rural Bangladesh', *Lancet*, 5 November, vol. 2, pp. 946-8.

People (1975a), 'Clean slate on injectables', vol. 2, issue 3, p. 28.

People (1975b), 'Injectables in Thailand' vol. 2, issue 2, p. 35.

Powell, L.C., and Seymour, R.J. (1971), *American Journal of Obstetrics and Gynaecology*, vol. 110, no. 36.

Quality of Health Care and Human Experimentation, US Senate Subcommittee hearings on (1973), evidence presented, and quoted by Gena Corea in *The Hidden Malpractice*, Morrow & Co., New York, 1977, pp. 153-6.

Rakusen, J. (1974), 'Information or Propaganda?', *Spare Rib*, no. 32, pp. 6-8, London.

Rinehart, W. and Winter, J. (1975), 'Injectables and implants', *Population Reports*, George Washington University Medical Center, March, series K, no. 1 (see p. K10).

Rosenfield, A. (1978), Professor of Obstetrics-Gynaecology and Public Health at Columbia University, testifying at the US Select Committee on Population, House of Representatives, August 8-10 (see Benagniano, 1978).

Savage, W. (1978), 'The use of Depo-provera in East London', *Fertility and Contraception*, July, vol. 2, no. 3, pp. 41-7.

Saxena, B.N., Shrimanker, K., Grudzinskas, J.G. (1977), *Contraception*, December, vol. 16, no. 6, p. 605.

Schwallie, P.C. and Mohberg, N.R. (1977), 'Medroxyprogesterone acetate: an injectable contraceptive', *Advances in Planned Parenthood*, vol. 12, no. 1, pp. 36-44.

Scutchfield, F.D., Long, W.N., Corey, B., Tyler, C.W. (1971), 'Medroxyprogesterone acetate as an injectable female contraceptive', *Contraception*, vol. 3, pp. 21-35.

Seitz, R. (1979), 'A Filipino push for Depo', *People*, vol. 6, issue 2, p. 32.

Smith, M. (1978), 'Depoprovera – a Review', *Scottish Medical Journal*, July, vol. 23, p. 3.

Toppozada, M. (1978), evidence to US Select Committee on Population, House of Representatives (see Benagniano, 1978).

Trussell, T.J., Faden, R., Hatcher, R.A. (1976), 'Efficacy Information in Contraceptive Counselling: Those Little White Lies', *American Journal of Public Health*, vol. 66, no. 8, p. 76.

Upjohn (1971), 'Effect on Lactation', *Depo-provera Research Newsletter*, 2.

Upjohn (1972a), 'Return of Fertility Following Discontinuance', *Depo-provera Research Newsletter*, 3.

Upjohn (1972b), 'Bleeding disturbances on Depo-provera and their management', *Depo-provera Research Newsletter*, 4.

Upjohn (1973), 'Those Wretched Beagles', *Depo-provera Research Newsletter*, 7.

Vecchio, T.J. (1972), 'Depo-provera – international experience in over 20,000 cases', *Journal of Reproductive Medicine*, vol. 8, no. 4, p. 208.

Vecchio, T.J. (1973), 'Injectable Medroxyprogesterone acetate contraception: metabolic and endocrine effects', *Journal of Reproductive Medicine*, vol. 10, pp. 193-6.

Vecchio, T.J. (1974), 'Long-acting injectable contraceptives', unpublished.

Vessey, M.P., Mears, E., Andolsek, L., Ogrinc-Oven, M. (1972), 'Randomised double-blind trial of four oral progestogen-only contraceptives', *Lancet*, 29 April, vol. 1, pp. 915-22.

Wilson, A. (1978), 'Bengali Women and the Health Service', *Poverty and Power*, vol. 1, issue 1, pp. 12-13.

Wilson, E. (1976), 'Use of long-acting depot progestogen in domiciliary family planning', *British Medical Journal*, 11 December, vol. 4, pp. 1435-7.

Wilson, E. (1979), personal communication.

Wyrick, R. (1979), 'Contraceptive Tied to Cancer', *Newsday*, 3 June.

Zanartu, J., Onetto, E., Medina, E., Dabancens, A. (1973), 'Mammary Gland Nodules in women under continuous exposure to progestogens', *Contraception*, vol. 7, issue 3, pp. 203-12.

5

Seizing the means of reproduction: an illegal feminist abortion collective – how and why it worked

Pauline Bart

This chapter provides an example of women – to use Barbara Ehrenreich and Deirdre English's (1974, p. 84) phrase – seizing 'the technology without buying the ideology'.

A stark contrast has always been drawn between legal abortions performed by white-coated physicians in accredited hospitals and clinics, and 'dirty back-alley' abortions performed by evil 'quacks'. This paper describes an alternative – abortions being performed illegally by laywomen who learned the procedures because of their feminist politics, their identification with women, and their belief that all women have the right to control their bodies. As well as being safe, the abortions were educational experiences for the women who needed them. They learned that health services could be offered at minimal cost in an unalienating way, and that the providers could be interested in more than the specific procedure, since the women were also given contraceptive counselling and pap smears, as well as literature such as Our Bodies Ourselves, The Birth Control Handbook, *and* The VD Handbook. *The women in this illegal organisation which was called The Service, or 'Jane', experienced what can best be described as a 'growth experience', coming to like themselves and other women more.*

Roth (1974) states that for many years we have been trying unsuccessfully to teach professionals to love their patients. He suggests, therefore, that we teach people who already love the patients the necessary professional and technical skills, a point also raised by Katy Gardner in her chapter on Well Woman clinics. The achievements of 'Jane' demonstrate the perceptiveness of this remark.

Attempts to tighten abortion legislation highlight the importance of a serious consideration of solutions that go further than mere protest. As Pauline Bart writes, the situation will never go back to the way it was before 'Jane'. Now there are feminist health centres throughout the USA. So not only are there people who believe a woman has a right to control her body, but, more importantly, they also have the skills to ensure that she keeps that right either legally or illegally. They can give us laws, they can take away laws. But they can't take away skills.

In her chapter, based on her research on an abortion service provided by women and for women, Bart looks at who the women were, how the service worked and why, and concludes by looking at the positive effects of the service on the women running it, as well as on the women needing abortions.

That the standard method of delivery of health care is not meeting the medical needs of large sectors of the population has been demonstrated often enough to need no further documentation. The very term itself – *delivery* – usually refers to *objects* and to apply it to something as dependent on inter-personal relationships as health care, signifies that those who name (and Mary Daly (1979) has pointed out the importance of the power to name) see little difference between delivering pianos and what passes for health care. Indeed, within standard health institutions there may be very little difference, for so many professionals regard health care not as a process, but rather as a product. Inevitably, human beings are dehumanised, divided into many parts, and placed on an assembly line where the doctors have access to the most profitable parts. This reduction of human beings to their particular medical parts and the consequent control exercised by doctors over those parts (and thereby over human beings) is something that feminists have found most undesirable – on many counts – and have sought to change.

From the earliest days, one unifying demand within the women's movement has been to assert the unity and autonomy of those 'medical parts' and we have struggled for the control of our bodies (or, as I put it, we have aimed at seizing the means of reproduction). The Women's Health Movement, combining the tenets of the radical health movement and the feminist movement, is a response to this demand developed notably through the philosophy of self-help. By demystifying women's bodies, not only through educational efforts such as the fine book *Our Bodies Ourselves*, but directly and specifically through cervical self-examination, and by trying to decrease hierarchical relations between health workers in feminist health centres, the goal of control of our bodies and our selves is approached. While all women may not want to, or in fact cannot, be assistant professors or executives, all women have bodies and have to deal with the health care system. Thus an attempt to change this system and provide alternatives can benefit all women.

Abortion after legalisation

Nowhere is a woman's powerlessness to control her body more manifest than in the area of abortion. Legalisation has not solved all the problems. Abortions after the first three months of pregnancy are difficult to obtain, many hospitals do not perform abortions at all, particularly in rural areas, clinics performing out-patient abortions are harassed, and federal, state and local governments have instituted restrictions – particularly on third-party payments so that it is still difficult for poor women to obtain abortions. Recently, the American Medical Association won its struggle against the Feminist Women's Health Center in Tallahassee, Florida, which had been suing the Florida Medical Association for being a combination in restraint of trade (monopoly). The medical group had threatened and blackballed gynaecologists who performed abortions in the clinic, and therefore no local gynaecologist could be obtained. One can be justly suspicious of their rhetoric (allegedly good, safe, medical care), when one learns that the clinic charged much less than private physicians.[2]

When abortion was first legalised in some states (e.g. California), women had to obtain the consent of psychiatrists who testified that their mental health would be seriously damaged or that they would kill themselves if they did not obtain an abortion. Such degradation rituals are pithily expressed in a cartoon by pro-abortion activist Patricia McGinnis showing a sobbing woman with a $500 cheque in front of 'Mercy Hospital' saying, on her knees:

> 'Please may I have a state-approved, politician-sanctioned, clergy-counselled, psychiatrist-rubber-stamped, residency-investigated, abortion committee-inspected, therapuked, public health dept.-statistized, contraceptive-failure, accredited hospital abortion'.

So women were still powerless in the hands of certified professionals.

But before abortion was legalised, the situation was even worse, except for wealthy women who could always obtain abortions, if not in the USA, then in Japan or Scandinavia (although in Scandinavia they still had to be approved by a board). Every woman, if she herself had not had an abortion or even experienced the fear that she might be unwillingly pregnant, knew of a friend or relative who had had to search for an illegal abortionist and undergo pain and humiliation as well as expense. Complications from self-induced abortion, done primarily by poor women and young women, reached almost epidemic proportions in some places, not infrequently causing permanent damage. So it was not surprising that a great deal of energy went into changing abortion laws.

Denes (1976), studying a New York abortion hospital run for profit, shows the continuing alienation of women seeking abortion in the health system as it exists, and thus demonstrates the importance of learning from an alternative approach such as that which will be discussed below in our analysis of 'Jane'. Denes says the hospital is falling apart in terms of morale, not because of economic factors but rather 'because of its relationship to death'. She was told by the staff 'that one has to make a living but otherwise who *would* such burdens bear' (243) (feminists in 'Jane' in Chicago, as will be shown, and in Europe, would). She continues by describing the hierarchical arrangements in the hospital and the misogyny of the gynaecologists, one of whom admitted (ibid., 227):

> 'Basically every gynaecologist doesn't like women, otherwise he couldn't work with them. The fact is that he is the god, king, they do what he tells them, which is what he would always want women to do, because every man wants his women subservient to him.'

The nurses refused to be interviewed. Denes (or, as she was addressed in the book, 'Dr Denes') noted that women were having abortions because of pressure from their boyfriends, and she remarked on the 'bureaucratic banality of suffering' as she observed a woman needing an abortion sign a seemingly unending flow of consent forms.

But the problem is not inherent in the abortion procedure, as Denes claims. Women having abortions with 'Jane' were thoroughly counselled so that those who didn't really want them would have had an opportunity not to go through with the procedure. In fact, about one quarter of the women did not return after counselling. Needless to say, in an illegal procedure no consent forms were signed. Moreover hierarchical relationships were minimised. There was no misogyny. What Denes should have said is that the problem is inherent in the way medical care is traditionally 'delivered'.

'Jane'

In 1969, some women living in Hyde Park, around the University of Chicago, many of whom had been in the peace and civil rights movement and/or liberal politics, first began to develop some feminist consciousness, stimulated in part by the organising of the Chicago Women's Liberation Union. It seemed logical to them to counsel women and help them obtain illegal abortions. There was an informal referral service operating from a University of Chicago dorm by a student who wanted a group to take it over. At that time, no one thought that they themselves would be doing the abortions or even that the men they thought were physicians were in fact illegal abortionists. They negotiated from a power position, promising the abortionists clients if they would do a percentage of abortions free for poor women and if they could get feedback from the women about the quality of the service offered. The abortionists were taken aback, since they were used to dealing with powerless, terrified women, but they consented. During its four years of operation (1969-73) 'Jane' proved that abortions can be performed safely, humanely and very inexpensively by non-professional paramedics working in apartments. As one woman, the first 'Jane' abortionist, and one of the charismatic leaders wrote:

> In spite of the fact that women who came through our abortion service were largely women who had nowhere else to go – too far pregnant, too poor, too young, too oppressed, too sick, too alone; and in spite of having to work under incredible stress, with inadequate facilities and no cloak of legitimacy to protect us, our medical results over four years compare favourably with the results of licensed medical facilities in New York and California.
>
> During the first eighteen months, the responsibility of the women in the service evolved from counselling and referring, then to medically assisting established abortionists and finally to doing the entire procedure.
>
> We learned to give shots, to take blood pressure, to take and read pap smears for cancer. We performed abortions on pregnant 11-year-olds and on pregnant 50-year-olds.
>
> We learned to do a D and C – standard dilation and

curettage – and to use a vacuum aspirator for the operation.

We learned from identifying and understanding feelings in our own bodies and then trying to relate them to another woman's problems and feelings.

When women in the service became able to provide all services from counselling to midwifing induced abortions, we reached a new stage of autonomy and a new level of politics. Our first move was to drop the price, and the bottom fell out of the abortion black market.

But learning and becoming self-sufficient was not an overnight process. While the abortionist was still taking responsibility for medical procedures, we were learning other skills: how to deal with doctors and hospitals, how to talk to the police, how to buy drugs and instruments, how to counsel more effectively, how to recruit and train new counsellors, and how to maintain democracy, efficiency and sisterhood among a group of women.

Counsellor, patient or paramedic – we were all partners in the crime of demanding the freedom to control our own bodies and our own childbearing.

She told me that she did not use the term 'patient'

'because patient is a word that the medical establishment uses. To me it implies a subject-object relation and we always tried to get away from thinking of the women who came through the service as objects we were going to do something to.'

Obtaining permission to study the group was difficult. They said it was ironic for a group that was anti-professional and anti-academic to be studied by an academic. They were not concerned (with one exception) about their illegal activities becoming known because seven of them had been arrested and the charges had been dismissed, following the Supreme Court's decision to legalise abortion. Moreover, now the consensus of the group is that the police had known what they were doing, and had not intervened (the 'bust' was a mistake) since 'Jane' was providing a necessary service for policemen's wives, mistresses and daughters and for policewomen. Unlike other illegal abortionists they didn't leave bleeding bodies in motels for the police to have to fill out forms on and deal with. When charges were dropped against the seven who were arrested, they believed that it was because Chicago did not want another political trial.

I promised the women that they could have input into any monograph I would write and that any royalties I received would be put back into the Women's Movement. I didn't have a grant (which they considered proof of my not being co-opted), I had been involved in feminist activities in Chicago, and they did not perceive my demeanour as 'professional'. Therefore, some of the key women decided to trust me, other women were told, and, for the most part after that, I had no difficulty obtaining interviews. Some women even called asking to be interviewed. *Everyone* I asked, including women who were originally reluctant, ultimately spoke with me.

I talked with every woman who did more than counselling (with the exception of one or two women who had moved to places like Hawaii and Nebraska that I couldn't get to in the course of my travels). I did interview women in Oakland, California, Washington, D.C., and Boston, and I interviewed all the counsellors I could locate.

Not only did I have no refusals but no one missed an interview. They would always notify me if they could not make their appointments, in one instance calling me long distance. This behaviour demonstrates the high degree of responsibility which indeed we would expect from women who would voluntarily risk their freedom to enable other women to keep theirs.

Since this is retrospective research, the data collected are remembrances of things past, and, in certain instances, there is a divergence of opinion. When I discovered different perceptions and interpretations, I addressed questions to issues such as: Was 'Jane' a collective? Was 'Jane' responsible for the one woman who died? (she arrived septic). I also addressed questions dealing with different attitudes: Is abortion murder? (not the exact wording of the question). The interviews lasted anywhere from 45 minutes (with women who only counselled and were not involved in the interpersonal politics) to 2 hours, with a return visit for some of the more central women, particularly those who did everything, and for the early interviews when I didn't know what to ask. Almost all the interviews were conducted at the women's homes which furnished me with additional data on their way of being in the world, and helped me to understand them better.

Who were the women?

The ideology of 'Jane' is that they are just ordinary women – not superwomen. An examination of their demographics clearly demonstrates that this is not the case. They are highly educated and predominantly middle class. Over half the group state that they have more energy than the people they know, while only two say they have less. Eight need six or fewer hours' sleep per night. They entered 'Jane' primarily through friendship networks, or because they or their friends had abortions with The Service. That a number of women entered via that route validates my impression, and their belief, that the abortions were in fact satisfactory experiences for the clients. Prospective members attended three meetings during which they learned how to counsel first and second trimester women, the physiology of abortion and the workings of 'Jane'. How much was disclosed to them varied with the 'paranoia' of the women presenting the information. At the beginning, some were not told that the abortionists were not medically qualified. Later, some of them were not told that the women themselves were performing the procedures. There was some resentment among the women that they were not trusted. On the other hand one can understand the dilemma. Since the women were not screened, it was unclear how much to trust them. But, to be effective counsellors, they had to have a maximum of knowledge. Usually the decision was made to trust. Only once did a woman (a reporter) deliberately infiltrate simply to write a story which, although names were not given, made the collective very frightened and very angry. It was not until much later that they realised that the police were not interested in stopping them.

Because long-terms (women more than three months' pregnant) had different procedures than first trimesters, they were given different counselling. Birth control information was given and the women received copies of *Our Bodies Ourselves*, *The Birth Control Handbook*, and *The VD Handbook*.

One 'Jane' member described the counselling procedure as follows:

> 'The basic information was the description depending on how many weeks they were. You either do a description of a D & C or a description of the miscarriage. In the long-term you had to do both because we had to do the D & C after the miscarriage. Some people didn't want to hear it but I went through it all anyway every time. I always used to convey the idea that it was going to hurt on the theory that if it didn't hurt it would be a relief and if it did hurt it would be no surprise.'

I asked her how she knew if the woman had emotional problems that she needed to discuss regarding the abortion. She responded:

> 'I guess you would have to watch it and it all depended on (to me) the woman. Some women would start to interrupt right away and they wanted to talk about how they felt and then if they would start to run down I would start to drag in this body of information I had to give them. Some people would just sit there mute and I would just talk and at the end I would say "Have you thought about it?" Some people didn't want to talk to you about how they felt in which case I tended to leave it alone after I made a few stabs at it.'

The counselling was considered the heart of the procedure

and it was believed that you could tell by the woman's response during the abortion if she had not been well counselled.

The one woman who died had managed to avoid being counselled, presumably because she was frightened that the counsellor would learn that she had had an incomplete abortion and refuse her the procedure. She was told she would be counselled at *The Front* (described below, p. 120). Women learned to counsel as they learned all the skills, primarily through an apprenticeship system (in addition to the orientation session). They were assigned a *Big Sister* whose counselling sessions they sat in on. Then the Big Sister sat in with them.

How did it work?

1 A woman needing an abortion would obtain the phone number of 'Jane' from the Chicago Women's Liberation Union, personal networks or sometimes even from local police officers. She would then call, hear a taped message starting 'This is "Jane" ' and be told to leave her name and number.

2 The tapes would be picked up every 2 hours and the call would be returned by a woman assigned to that task (called *Callback Jane*) who would take a medical history and say that a counsellor would call. Women who worked on Callback Jane (which became one of the paid jobs) had to have free telephone time, and thus women with small children who would interrupt conversations could not hold that job.

3 The woman needing the abortion would be assigned to a counsellor by the administrator (another paid job and one which was unpopular) who was called *Big Jane*. (Once two women split this job.) Big Jane assigned the woman to a counsellor to whom she gave the medical information.

4 The counsellor would see the woman either individually or in a group, depending on her preference. Everybody counselled so that their work would always be grounded

in the woman's experience. One abortionist did not counsel and her failure to do so was thought to be the cause of her inadequate performance. She was ultimately 'fired'. Counselling was primarily demystification, the woman being told exactly what to expect. Intrapsychic factors were not dealt with unless the woman seemed to need to address these issues. One key person said that it was condescending to ask the woman if she were sure she wanted an abortion, but that she might be asked if she had told her mother or what would happen if she didn't have the abortion. In a group setting the women would offer support to one another.

5 Big Jane would contact the counsellor and give her the appointment time, date, and address where the woman was to go. She would then inform the woman.

6 The woman would go to an apartment called '*The Front*' with significant other(s) of her choice. The Front, which was set up for security reasons, was described by one interviewer as 'a mob scene' and another said 'working the front' (one of the jobs) was a 'very heavy job'. Another woman said it was 'like being a stewardess with a radical feminist consciousness'. Women were offered comfort, orange juice, tea and coffee, and sometimes politics.

7 The women, but not their significant others, were taken by the 'Jane' worker who was driving that day to an apartment where the procedure was done. The entire process, including a pap smear, took 3 hours, although a first trimester abortion took only 10-15 minutes.

8 They were brought back by car to The Front where they were reunited with their friends, boyfriends etc.

9 The woman was supposed to be in phone contact with her counsellor for a week. If she didn't call, the counsellor would call her.

10 The process for second trimester, or 'long-term', abortions varied. Either Leumbach Paste was inserted or the amniotic sac was ruptured or the umbilical cord was cut to induce labour.[3] Then the woman was given careful instructions on how to deal with the hospital, what her rights were and what she didn't have to tell them. When

the women were 'hassled' in spite of that information, a midwifery apartment was set up with 'Jane' women who specialised in delivering 'long-terms'.

It should be noted that a major logistical problem was disposal of the 'products of conception' (embryos and foetuses). At night, 'runs' were made to supermarket disposal bins. On one occasion a foetus was found but was not traced to 'Jane'. Men sometimes assumed this task.

So far I have mentioned the following roles in 'Jane' counsellor; Big Jane; Callback Jane; driver; woman who 'worked The Front'; first trimester and long-term abortionists. Women also acted as assistants giving injections, inserting speculums and dilating cervixes. All these jobs, except abortionist, were present when there were male abortionists. One of the male abortionists taught one of the women and she taught the others, enabling them to eliminate the professional 'for profit' abortionists, flatten the hierarchy (there is some disagreement on how flat it actually was), perform free or very low cost abortions and pay some of the workers.

The emergent dominant political philosophy was feminist-anarchist so that all women were called paramedics and all women tried to do everything. Not all women wanted to assist and fewer wanted to do abortions, either because of lack of time, commitment, interest, or skill (though remember all women counselled). The ideology was that everyone could do everything. It was thought good for the women they were doing the procedures with to see the 'Jane' women change jobs, since it demonstrated to these women that the skills were not mystical but were easily transferable. As one woman movingly put it, in what I consider one of the most important expressions of the 'Jane' experience and of the philosophy of self-help:

> 'If it's necessary you can take the tools of the world in your own hands, and all that crap about how you have to be expert to do anything, whether fixing your car or your vacuum cleaner or administering medical aid is just a ruse to make you feel incompetent in your

own life. *One thing we all learned is that if you want to learn how to do something you can do it.*'

Why did it work?

The major question I wanted to answer in this study of 'Jane', in fact the reason why I wanted to do this research, was to learn why it worked, not only to make a contribution to sociological theory, but because such data would have important implications for social policy. While I learned a number of reasons which accounted for 'Jane's' effectiveness when other groups with equally good will floundered, many of the reasons are historically unique.

The social and historical context

The brutality at the Democratic Convention in Chicago in 1968 radicalised the Hyde Park Chicago and liberal and radical communities, leaving them angry and disenchanted with existing institutions. The 1960s was a time of change. People were involved not only in political change, but also in changing their life-styles and seeking new experiences. One 'Jane' woman told me The Service would not have been possible at other times. It was in this climate that the Women's Movement began to attain momentum in Chicago (the first national Women's Liberation meeting was held in Chicago at the end of 1967). While many of the 'Jane' women were not feminists to begin with and some were not even political at all, they did want to do something for and with women. Such opportunities were more limited then than they are now. Since this was their first feminist activity they had an enormous amount of energy, faith and hope as well as a great deal of anger against men and patriarchal institutions. One woman said 'This was *our* issue. It wasn't our men's and it wasn't our kids' schools. It was ours and the energy was terrific.' They had not yet been 'burnt out'. At first no one questioned sisterhood since no one had been betrayed by another feminist. These factors fuelled the enormous amount of energy they put into 'Jane'. A professional feminist organiser and former 'Jane' woman told me:

> 'the . . . rage was hard to deal with but it led to the making of a tremendous commitment of time and energy. It was just something that clicked because you were working with your friends and you were recruited by friendship so there was a tremendous commitment to each other as well as to the issues and to the clients.'

Charismatic leaders

There was general agreement on who the leaders were and that they were enormously talented and competent. Not everyone liked all of them though. The original key people were primarily housewives which enabled them to devote the time necessary to organise The Service before there were paying jobs for the women. Today most women like that would be employed, but at that time educated competent women could still be found at home, supported by their husbands.

The illegality

Although 'energy' was lost due to 'paranoia', engaging in illegal activities made the group cohesive. More importantly, the illegality made it absolutely necessary to do the abortions since the services they provided were not replaceable. If they did not do it, the women needing the procedures would have no satisfactory alternatives. One of the charismatic leaders stated: 'The illegal is the crux of it – the fact that it is illegal made it override all the other political discrepancies – swept all of us together. It made it seem political when it wasn't.'

The big step towards their perception of its illegality was not the referral service and not doing it themselves. Rather it was learning that the abortionists were not physicians. After that knowledge had been accepted, following a great deal of discussion at their meetings, it was only a small step to doing it themselves. After all, if being a doctor was not a prerequisite for doing good abortions, why shouldn't they? It is ironic to note that the physicians didn't receive training in how to do abortions in medical school, since abortions were illegal. Performing a D. and C., which they learned, is not the same as performing an abortion. It should also be noted that, because of the civil rights and peace movements in which many of the women had participated and which were heavily concentrated in Hyde Park where 'Jane' started, there was a tradition of civil disobedience to unjust laws. No one with whom I spoke had any moral problems about violating abortion laws although some were frightened by the illegality. Interestingly, there emerged a continuum of attitudes towards illegality – some women were frightened, some ignored it, and some liked the danger. Moreover, the fact that they operated an illegal system made for more efficiency. No time had to be spent 'hassling' with licensing agencies and filling out forms. (Some of the women subsequently formed a woman's health centre, where they found such restrictions very constraining.)

The importance of, and satisfaction derived from, enabling women to have abortions

In contrast to other groups of people with equal good will, the women in 'Jane' could actually solve problems. A woman would walk in pregnant and leave no longer pregnant. Moreover, as another woman put it,

> 'whenever there were personal problems or political disagreements they were always subordinated to the job in hand, because abortion was not something one could have political disagreements about . . . no matter how much people had different politics in their work, middle class housewives who were members of NOW and women who were radical hippie freaks, dopers, women from the Union (the Chicago Women's Liberation Union – socialist feminists) and who knows what else. There were students and non-students. . . . But it could never matter because ultimately you had to do

> the abortion. You can argue a real lot about demonstrations, you can argue a real lot about posters, you can argue a real lot about canvassing, you can argue a real lot about what you're writing in your leaflets, but you can't argue about doing an abortion, you're going to do it or you're not and if you're going to then you do it.'

Some women mentioned that it was the very absence of a 'correct political line' (except on abortion) that enabled the group to survive and continue to be effective.

Financial self-sufficiency

A final reason for 'Jane's' success, and one that is directly relevant for other groups, is the fact that The Service supported itself and could pay salaries. While it was norm-violating for workers to be involved simply for money, the fact that women could be paid enabled a group of women to put a great deal of time into The Service who otherwise would have had to have what they termed 'shit jobs'. They were enabled to lead totally radical feminist lives. In addition, it ended the contradiction some women felt about 'Jane' women being supported by their husbands. Moreover, no energy had to go into fund-raising (except for the defence fund when the women were 'busted'). Those familiar with alternative institutions know, the amount of time that goes into obtaining funds, into grant-writing and into unending debates about whether taking such funds means co-option.

Before concluding, it is worthwhile to look at the effect of 'Jane' on some of the participants. A number of women, particularly the older ones, had already become disillusioned with the health care system, frequently around their childbirth experiences, but now all of them have real contempt for the system. Even one woman who is currently a medical student said, 'I will share any skill I learn with anyone who wants to learn it. If someone wants to know how to do open-heart surgery and I have learned how, I'll teach it to them.'

For me, the most moving experience was learning how

participating in 'Jane' improved the women's self-image and their view of other women, as well as giving them skills which enable them to have more control over their lives. One elementary school teacher said:

> 'When I joined the feminist movement someone said to me, "scratch any woman deep enough and you are going to find a feminist". And being involved in Jane especially in the counselling part where one has to talk to many women and being up in The Front I found that under the skin it didn't matter if you were big or black or white or green or small or fat or rich or poor. Women had to deal with the same problems and it radicalized me in that respect. I truly believe this now I feel that tremendous kinship to women and I find that I seek out women as opposed to men, . . . but the thing that was the most interesting with my husband was that he suddenly gained a better insight into this because when we first started we thought that only poor black women were going to come and he saw people coming to our house and they were all kinds of people and all ages of people and this to him was radicalizing too. . . . I also learned how my body functioned and that was to me one of the best things and I think I also learned about how to demand services from the medical profession because I knew about my body I could now say, "hey, listen . . . what's happening, tell me" . . . and I didn't take any of this little crap stuff that doctors were giving, I wasn't their little girl and I don't know if this was "Jane", if this was the feminist movement or being involved in NOW, I don't know. I do know though that it changed my whole outlook about myself. . . .'

Not only did it affect the women who were in The Service, but they believed, probably correctly, that it affected the women who went through as clients. A woman who is now a day-care organiser said:

> 'Well one of the things that I thought was extraordinary

about the service was the effect that it had on the women that went through it. Seemed to me that part of what was extraordinary about the service was the way in which, because we were providing an immediate concrete service, we were able to bring up questions in people's minds about so many things about the medical profession. About their own oppression. About the institutions of a society that were wreaking havoc on their lives. It certainly seemed like we were turning a lot of people's heads around. . . . I don't know that it was what we said as much as what we did. It was a political experience and we talked about it. Almost everyone asked if their abortionist was a doctor. It seemed like it was politically important to be able to say that he was not, she was not and to be able to say that some of the people who were doing the abortions were members of The Service who had learned how to do it. But that meant we had to create faith in them, confidence in their competence and that abortion was something that people could learn how to do without being a male who'd gone through 4 years' medical school. Sometimes people, I guess, probably just endured it because they were in a trouble situation and this was their only option, but sometimes, I think, it made an impression on people and even more made an impression when they went through the experience, found out we used and we made a point to have, these bright coloured striped flowered sheets and painted the rooms green and blue, nice colours, that how comfortable and homey it was. How nice it was not to be up on a table with your legs up in the stirrups and all the white all over the place. It seemed like it was setting an example showing people that medical experiences didn't have to be in the traditional mode.'

This study demonstrates that the belief that only doctors can perform safe abortions is incorrect. It also shows the limits of the current ideology promulgated by the human potential movement, that people 'grow' by focusing on themselves and their own perceived needs rather than on other people and their needs. We sometimes call this ideology 'growthspaceautonomy' and have pointed out that it can function as a legitimation of psychopathy. After all cancer is also growth. The dichotomy between taking care of others and taking care of oneself is false. In fact it was precisely by taking care of others, the women who needed abortions, that the women in The Service most frequently fulfilled their own potential.

Notes

1 Another version of this chapter is forthcoming in *Social Problems*. A chapter dealing with the psychological changes in the women, their self-esteem, and their increased feelings of competence will appear in *Workplace Democracy and Social Change*, ed Frank Lindenfield and Joyce Rothschild-Witt (Porter Sargent, Boston), under the title 'Collective Work and Self Identity: the Effect of Working in a Feminist Illegal Abortion Collective', Melinda Bart Schlesinger and Pauline Bart.

2 Since this chapter was written there has been a further development in this case. Although the Feminist Women's Health Center case was lost in Tallahassee, the Appeals judge in New Orleans sent it back to Tallahassee for a retrial. The Medical Association decided to settle out of court.

3 Anyone seeking a second trimester abortion should be aware of the risks attached to these methods [Ed.].

References

Boston Women's Health Collective (1976), *Our Bodies, Ourselves*, Simon & Schuster, New York.

Daly, Mary (1979), *Gyn/ecology: The Metaethics of Radical Feminism*, Beacon Press, Boston.

Denes, Magda (1976), *In Necessity and Sorrow: Life and Death in an Abortion Hospital*, Penguin, New York.

Ehrenreich, Barbara and Deirdre English (1974), *Complaints and Disorders: The Sexual Politics of Sickness*, Compendium, London.

Roth, Julius (1974), 'Care of the Sick: Professionalism vs Love', *Social Science and Medicine*, vol 1, no. 3, April, pp. 173-80.

6

Well Woman clinics:

a positive approach to women's health

Katy Gardner

The area of reproduction represents immense contradictions. Although reproduction is a 'natural' event – indeed what could be more natural than reproducing the species? – medical men have progressively medicalised and technologised childbirth and extended control over birth control and abortion, turning reproduction from a 'normal' into an 'abnormal' event.

This chapter, like Pauline Bart's on seizing the means of reproduction, describes a positive step women have taken. Instead of treating women as sick when they go to the doctor, Katy Gardner suggests what we might do, and just what medical care could be like, if women were treated as well.

Herself a General Practitioner running a Well Woman clinic, Gardner looks at the possibilities for positive change within the National Health Service. She describes the work of different types of Well Woman clinic, and the services offered, Of course, even if we start from the premise that women are not 'sick', we must recognise that large numbers of women suffer and die from forms of cancer which could, it is argued, be treated if detected at an early stage.

In common with other contributions, the following describes the lack of access women have to knowledge about their own bodies. Katy Gardner sees the Well Woman clinic as a forum for the provision of such knowledge and argues that such facilities should be available to all women.

The National Health Service in Great Britain has a unique system of health care relying on the General Practitioner as the gateway to other services, with a more recent emphasis on the GP as a family doctor working with a health care team providing whole person health care. From this we should expect that the NHS should be prevention-based and orientated towards the community. But this is not so – Why? Because the medical profession has always been disease-orientated, because the medical profession has taken control of 'health' and because, for reasons of finance and power, the medical profession is reluctant to change the present orientation.

Medical treatment has often been assumed to be responsible for the great advances in standards of health in the last 100 years, but there is no doubt that the main advances have been made by better nutrition and public health and hygiene. After all, it is well established that medical treatment in the form of the hospitalisation of childbirth in the nineteenth century resulted in *increased* mortality for mothers and babies, before Semmelweiss discovered sepsis and transmission of infection.

Throughout medical history women have been battling with the medical profession for control of our bodies. Women are the major consumers of health care because:

1 at present we assume the main responsibility for contraception;
2 women encounter the medical profession during pregnancy and childbirth;
3 we still assume prime responsibility for well and sick children;
4 women's anatomy seems more complex than men's and

more likely to involve us in health problems and illness;
5 traditionally women have been seen as frail and doctors have capitalised on women's weaknesses by inventing treatments, for 'the vapours', etc. Although the day of the vapours has gone, women still see themselves as ill more often than men – men who are distressed may go to the pub – women go to the doctor.

I feel strongly that in general practice, especially with the establishment of health centres and care teams, the NHS potentially has the ability to provide a service which will meet the needs and demands of women.

Given the above, the concept of the Well Woman clinic is an important one. I do not see Well Woman clinics as an attempt to further medicalise women's lives (Illich, 1975) but rather as an attempt to provide an open access system where any woman can go to have a check-up and discuss matters concerning her health and well-being with sympathetic health workers.

We should be aiming for an NHS where Well Woman clinics are provided as part of the routine service of general practice and primary care, but while we have a situation where 86 per cent of GPs are men and most patients are women, Well Woman clinics are a tactical necessity for which we should be fighting today. They are particularly necessary in inner city areas where many GPs practice 9-5-lock-up, pen-pushing medicine, and are not interested in the so-called 'trivia', which include problems such as vaginal discharges, period pains, menopausal problems, cystitis, all of which are far more relevant to women's everyday lives than 'diseases' as taught by hospitals and all of which can be crippling and devastating. By introducing women to a caring service we can increase their expectations of health care and, in this way, Well Woman clinics can bring pressure to bear on the medical profession to provide a decent service for women.

I do not see Well Woman clinics as an alternative to self-help groups or to women at work and at home organising to fight for a better service, but as an integral part of the struggle. Basically the aims of Well Woman clinics should be (and this represents a more ideal and radical view of their functions than most provide at present):

1 to reach women who normally stay clear of doctors for class or cultural reasons, or who are intimidated by male doctors, or whose doctors are not interested in such matters;
2 to teach women about self-help breast examination, remedies for thrush, prevention of cystitis (up to 80 per cent of women can be helped by simple preventative measures);
3 to screen women for cancer of the breast, cervix, ovary etc.;
4 to function as a sympathetic referral agency for any problems that come up (e.g. menorrhagia (heavy periods));
5 to raise the consciousness of women about health care: to put pressure on the medical profession to improve their service for women;
6 to publicise themselves through Community Health Councils, women's groups and trade unions;
7 to be involved in health education – especially in getting together local group discussions about health;
8 to train personnel – nurses, doctors and paramedical workers – in the procedures of Well Woman examination and especially in the concept of self-help and prevention. I see no reason why women who are not nurses or doctors but who have a basic training in dealing with health problems relating to women, could not perform a Well Woman examination and for that matter do a cancer smear test and provide some family planning services, such as prescribing the Pill. This has been done successfully in China, Sweden and Tanzania. My only hesitation is that we should be careful that such women do not become a cheap way out for the NHS.

I shall now outline three types of Well Woman clinics about which I have some knowledge. As one of the fundamental requisites of a local clinic is that it should be responsive to local needs these should not be seen as prescriptive but as possible ways of organising clinics:

1 Well Woman clinics in general practice;
2 Area Health Authority clinics in Islington;
3 Women's National Cancer Control Campaign clinics.

Having outlined possibilities I shall then briefly discuss cancer of the breast and cervix, because I believe that this is where women and the medical profession need to get together so that the benefits of Well Woman clinics can be brought home to the medical profession in general.

Well Woman clinics in general practice

Our practice aims to provide a reasonable level of care for women who come for whatever reason. If we are doing this, why have a separate Well Woman clinic? The reasons are partly political and partly practical. Two main reasons are: first, that having a separate clinic underlines for the women in our practice that we are concerned with 'health' as well as illness. We advertise the clinic 'Come for a chat and a check' in that order. Second, having a set clinic with 20 minutes at least of nurse and doctor's time per person allows time for us all to talk, be it about cystitis, pre-menstrual tension, the baby's teething troubles or whatever. The clinic has been going for 12 months with two doctors and a nurse seeing women from two practices in our health centre. An extremely important function of our clinic has been to teach the nurse how to do pelvic and breast examinations (she was previously doing smear tests only) so that all three of us are now more or less interchangeable. I have always been certain that any non-medical or paramedical person can do Well Woman examinations, provided they have some basic training in examination, know something about self-help for common conditions, and know how to be sympathetic, ask the right questions and refer problems with which they cannot cope. We take a full medical history as well as chatting about problems. Because women are 'patients' in the practice we can treat or deal with any problems (such as thrush, for example) which come up. Our physical examination is similar to that done by the Islington Well Woman Clinic described below. The women also get a cup of tea and there is a large selection of books for people to read and borrow. We very much want to have group discussion as part of the session but at present have not found a way round women having to wait if they all arrive at the same time initially.

Finally, each week we send for three women from our practice who have not had smears for more than 5 years according to our records. This is an attempt to reach women who do not normally come to Well Woman clinics – women who are often putting up with a lot, not wanting to 'bother' the doctor, and who may be at special risk for cervical cancer (women at greatest risk of this disease are the least likely to come for smears). It is often difficult to track these women down as we have a very mobile population living in inner Liverpool, but we are trying, and our nurse visits women who have not come after being sent for. Most of the women who have turned up have been really pleased that someone is actually bothering about their health and wanting to know if they have any problems.

Sometimes people level the criticism that Well Woman clinics will make women 'neurotic' about health. My experience indicates that this is not the case; one of our prime functions is to make health care friendly and informal and to enable women to get an idea of the standard of care they should expect and demand as a right. A recent survey of patients in central London general practices showed 80 per cent were broadly satisfied with their GP's care. Given the current state of many inner city practices this is a sad reflection of expectations of health care and one which will have to change if the NHS is to be made responsive to women's needs.

Islington Well Woman clinic

A few years ago a group of women from Islington Trades Council, Essex Road Women's Centre, and the National

Abortion Campaign, together with the local Community Health Council began a campaign for Well Woman clinics in Islington. This was a radical response to the situation in inner London where many GPs are elderly, have 'lock-up' surgeries, and, it could be said have little interest in examining patients at all – let alone 'well women'. The clinics were also aimed at increasing women's awareness of their health and health needs in order to voice a demand for a better standard of health care in Islington.

The Health Education Council was approached and various leaflets were drawn up about cystitis, the menopause, and so on. These leaflets also advertised the clinics and were displayed in shops and libraries. The Well Woman clinics are open access clinics operating once weekly in 5 welfare and health centres in Islington. They see only ten women per session, thereby giving time for discussion of problems, and have been so popular that the waiting lists vary (unfortunately) between 6 and 13 weeks. Every woman is seen by a health visitor first, who asks her history and tests urine and blood pressure. Then she is seen by the doctor who does a breast examination (with teaching of self-examination) and abdominal and pelvic examination, including a cancer smear test and swabs if necessary. At all times the woman is encouraged to discuss any problems she has, and, although the doctor does not offer treatment, she may refer the woman to her GP, or perhaps to a social worker, marriage guidance counsellor, family planning clinic or housing department, depending on what the problem is. The woman may be asked to return on another occasion. All personnel in these Well Woman clinics are women. The Islington clinics do not have any group discussion and doctors and health visitors work in conventional roles – although co-operatively as a team. But, despite the conventional aspect, they are very popular in providing a situation in which women can have time to air their fears and ask questions as well as being examined in a caring manner. For every woman screened the NHS cost is £7.44 (not very expensive and this includes a cancer smear).

What the Islington clinics do not do is call up women 'at risk' for screening (this again is where General Practitioners can come in useful) and one feels it will take some time before the news of these clinics spreads to those who may need them most. However, I feel they are providing a useful and popular service to women from all over North London, and, importantly, are open to *any* women in the UK who wishes to attend.[1] At present the clinics have the full support of local GPs.

Women's National Cancer Control Campaign

The Women's National Cancer Control Campaign (WNCCC)[2] is a charity and is an important example of a non-professional organisation which, over the last few years, has campaigned effectively with trade unions and Community Health Councils to provide a Well Woman screening service and health education service for many women throughout the country. The aims of the WNCCC are:

1. to provide a screening service for women who usually miss out – women at work, women in inner city areas, women of minority groups with language difficulties and so on;
2. to provide health education about cancer, primarily by means of leaflets, posters, TV and radio, co-operating closely with Area Health Authorities and using local media for publicity;
3. to promote local involvement in Well Woman screening in many areas up and down the country.

The WNCCC has worked with many trade unions to bring health care and screening into factories. For example, the Union of Shop Distributive and Allied Workers (USDAW) has invited WNCCC to screen its members nationwide and has contributed funds to the charity. The WNCCC will only go to an area if invited by a company (usually via trade union pressure) or Area Health Authority (often due to pressure from a Community Health Council). It provides its own equipment and mobile clinic and employs local NHS staff. All women are given blood pressure checks, breast and pelvic examinations and smear tests. Perhaps most important is the fact that they are given a chance to talk about their health problems. Where necessary they are referred to their local doctor or family planning clinic. I believe this is an example of how a body of non-medical people can act as a pressure group on the NHS. Sadly, it could also be seen as letting the NHS 'off the hook' by providing a service where the NHS does not.

Screening for breast cancer in Well Woman clinics[3]

Screening for breast cancer has been given much publicity in recent years and this is obviously something that Well Woman clinics should be doing. British United Provident Association (BUPA, a private health insurance agency) clinics provide mammography (X-ray scans of the breast) and other sophisticated tests at a price. This has led some women to demand an increase in the availability of such tests. However, the most recent evidence highlights the importance of regular self-examination as a means of detection of early breast cancer and an important function of Well Woman clinics is to explain and demonstrate this to women as well as explaining the 'ins and outs' of procedures and possibilities, if a breast lump is found.

Every year in the UK, 12,000 women die of breast cancer. One in seventeen women will get breast cancer at some stage in her life. Factors increasing risk include: family history of breast cancer; childlessness; late menopause; history of cysts and other breast lumps; history of cancer in the other breast. Of course the woman or her GP is the best person to know if she is at risk. There is evidence that mammography may be useful in high risk cases but, in general, I believe regular self-examination is the best way to detect breast lumps. Once every 3 months is suggested as a reasonable interval.

Mammography can produce false positive and false negative results and, if performed often, may itself induce cancer! Thermography (heat picture of the breast) is safe but very unreliable (20 – 30 per cent false positives and negatives), so we come back to simple self-examination. Recent studies have shown that this is more likely to detect really early cancer (at a stage when cure is a possibility) than even yearly examinations by an 'expert' at a Well Woman clinic.

The news that breast cancer can be detected early by self-examination is the best news we have had for a long time, because until now over 50 per cent of cancers detected by chance have spread by the time of presentation, and it is important to note that treatment has made *no* difference to the survival of women with breast cancer, although it may have removed some of the ugly consequences of the disease. Early detection seems to offer the best chance of survival and improvement in quality of life.

However, treatment for early breast cancer is *very* controversial. Basically, the options are:

1 'Lumpectomy' – removal of the lump only plus or minus radiotherapy (treatment by high intensity radiation to the affected part).
2 Simple mastectomy – removal of the breast, plus or minus radiotherapy, plus or minus removal of underarm glands.
3 Radical mastectomy – removal of chest muscle and breast and glands, plus or minus radiotherapy.
4 Modified radical mastectomy.

Surgeons are *not* objective about treatments, each favouring his or her own approach. Latest trials from the USA show that simple mastectomy has just as good results as radical mastectomy and that 'lumpectomy' may do just as well in the long-term though local recurrences (which can be treated with radiation) are more common. Who makes the decision about treatment? All too often it is the consultant bound by 'the system', which has resulted in some cases in women having mastectomies without understanding what was going on.

It is difficult for a woman to make an informed decision about what is best for her in view of all this confusion, but *every* woman with a lump that might be early cancer should have it removed and microscopically examined before undergoing further surgery; she should *insist* that no hasty decisions are made. This is where Well Woman clinics come in.

The staff of these clinics are used to dealing with these problems. They have more time to talk about consequences of mastectomy for a woman – What about her view of herself? What about prostheses (false breasts)? What is the best treatment for her as a person? And so on. They also have a role in counselling women about further advice and opinions, from the Royal Marsden Hospital (the expert cancer hospital in the UK) for instance, or the Mastectomy Association. Screening is only useful if it detects something that is worthwhile treating, and breast cancer is certainly painful and unpleasant if left to spread, but the consequences of screening must be dealt with so that every woman understands for herself what is happening.

Ninety-five per cent of breast lumps are 'benign' – that is, not cancer, but cysts or other simple lumps – and that is what we in Well Woman clinics impress upon women. It is always better to be safe than sorry. It is also better to be informed than at the mercy of 'experts'.

Cancer of the cervix (neck of the womb)

Well Woman clinics have an essential role to play in screening women for this disease – at present every year 17 million women are at risk and only 3 million women have smear tests. Every year, 2,400 women die of this cancer and two out of 1,000 women will develop it. This is perhaps not awfully common compared with breast cancer or even cancer of the ovary, but the latter is neither detectable early nor curable, whereas cancer of the cervix is both – or is it?

Over the last few years there has been a tremendous debate as to whether smear tests, which diagnose precancerous states as well as actual cancer, are helping to prevent cancer. Meanwhile, some women are having tests yearly and those at greatest risk usually never! (Women are very much at the mercy of GPs' whims, fancies and financial interests.) The number of new cases per year in young women is rising steadily – surely this is bad news? However, recent reports from Tayside and British Columbia indicate that when screening is carried out on *all* women, the incidence has actually fallen.

The likelihood of getting this cancer is related to certain factors, such as age at first sexual intercourse, number of partners, number of children and occupation of partners. While the incidence of cancer of the cervix in young women rises steadily, the Department of Health and Social Security only pays GPs to screen women over 35 or with 3 or more children (GPs ought to be doing these tests anyway, whether they are paid or not, but sadly money often seems more important to doctors than good medicine).

If we are going to screen by smear tests, when and who should we be screening? This is very controversial. The President of the British Society of Cytologists (the people who study the smears – a great deal of the value of the test depends on their expertise) recommends that every sexually active woman should have a smear at 20 and every 3 years thereafter until 65 and many experts agree with this. What of positive smears? A woman with a positive smear that is not overt cancer has a 30-60 per cent chance of developing cancer, over a period of years depending on her age. The older she is the greater the risk. The usual treatment of a positive smear, if it is positive when repeated, is a cone biopsy – removing a doughnut-shaped piece of the cervix which contains the abnormal cells. After this simple procedure, which has minimal side-effects, a woman has very little chance of a recurrence. If overt cancer is found in the biopsy, a hysterectomy and radiotherapy will usually be advised, with a high likelihood of cure. The following are the five-year survival rates for cancer of the cervix:

Microscopic cancer	90 per cent+
Extensive cancer with spread	15 per cent
Precancerous state, 'cancer *in situ*'	100 per cent

So the story is a hopeful one if smear tests become generally accepted for *all* women.

Even simpler procedures, which cause minimum inconvenience and discomfort, are now emerging to look at abnormal areas on the cervix (e.g., colposcopy – a technique using an operating microscope). Cryosurgery (freezing the affected areas off) and laser beam surgery are also now being used and do not usually require general anaesthetic. Follow-up for life is vital after all this, and should be the job of the Well Woman clinic or GP. Long trails to hospital and hours waiting for a quick smear and a wave at the doctor may make women give up.

Well Woman clinics have a vital role to play in publicising smear tests, explaining their value, advising on avoiding hazards (for instance, 'the cap' may protect women against cancer of the cervix as well as against thrush and sexually transmitted diseases), and explaining the consequences and significance of a positive smear. They also can give friendly counselling about the effects of possible treatments and the outlook for the woman's future.

Given this evidence on the beneficial and preventative role that Well Woman clinics can play in promoting the well-being of women, the question arises as to whether we should be campaigning for Well Woman clinics as a fundamental service provided by the NHS. We know their advantages and we must ask ourselves how we can best use this knowledge.

There are variations on this theme open to us. Should we be seeking woman-to-woman clinics as an alternative to general practice? Should we be insisting that more women become GPs to break down this male/expert, female/victim pattern of health service? Or should we be seeking wholesale change among GPs so that they can provide these Well Woman services within the existing structures of the NHS? Or, of course, should we be working on all these fronts in an attempt to ensure that, regardless of where the service is housed or administered, women have the maximum chance of being able to avail themselves of Well Woman facilities?

As both a GP and a woman, I sometimes find myself in a dilemma when it comes to suggesting the most positive course of action. But fundamentally, given the prevailing attitudes within society and within the medical profession, I feel that every woman should have the right to seek help at a clinic of her choice, run by women for women. In essence, this is what Well Woman clinics provide and why I think they should be readily available to all women.*

* *This chapter was written with much help, advice, assistance and typing from Pam Clarke.*

Notes for more information

1 Islington Community Health Council, Liverpool Road Hospital, Liverpool Road, London N1.
Well Woman Clinic, River Place Health Centre, Essex Road, London N1.
Bath Street Health Centre, London EC1.
Goodinge Health Centre, North Road, London N7.
Highbury Grange Health Centre, London N5.
North Islington Welfare Centre, Manor Gardens, London N7.
2 Women's National Cancer Control Campaign, 1 South Audley Street, London W1.
3 Tenovus Cancer Information Centre, 111 Cathedral Road, Cardiff CF1 9PH.
Mastectomy Association, 1 Colworth Road, Croydon, CR0 7AP.
Patients Association, Suffolk House, Banbury Road, Oxford.

References

General

Edwards, D. (1974), 'Gynaecological Abnormalities Found in a Cytology Clinic', *British Medical Journal*, vol. 49, pp. 218-21.

Ehrenreich, Barbara and Deirdre English (1979), *For Her Own Good: 250 Years of the Experts' Advice to Women*, Pluto Press, London. (Excellent *exposé* of the control of the medical profession over women and of the charlatan practices that have been perpetrated as 'medical treatment'.)

Illich, Ivan (1975), *Medical Nemesis: the Expropriation of Health*, Calder & Boyars, London. (Critique of medical practice from a Marxist perspective.)

Leeson, Joyce and Judith Gray (1978), *Women and Medicine*, Tavistock, London. (Comprehensive account of the relationship between women and the medical profession.)

Marsh G.N. (1976), 'Further nursing care in General Practice', *British Medical Journal*, vol. 3, pp. 626-8.

Breast and cervical cancer

Forrest, A.P.M. *et al.* (1980), 'Breast cancer screening', *British Journal of Hospital Medicine*, vol. 23, no. 1, pp. 8-21.

Foster, R.S. *et al.* (1978), 'Breast self examination practices and breast cancer', *New England Journal of Medicine*, vol. 299, pp. 265-76.

Kinlen, L.J. and A.I. Spriggs (1978), 'Women with positive cervical smears but without surgical intervention', *Lancet*, 26 August, pp. 463-5.

Last, Patricia (1979), 'The best place for screening women is in the GP's surgery', *Modern Medicine*, 19 April, pp. 25-8.

Singer, Albert (1977), 'Cancer of the Cervix', *Hospital Update*, October, pp. 553-65.

Taylor, R.W. (1979), 'Gynaecological malignancy', *Practitioner*, February, vol. 222, pp. 195-201.

7

A woman in medicine: reflections from the inside

Gail Young

Other chapters in this collection examine the control exercised over women by the medical profession in contexts where women are normally 'patients' and their medical advisers – the 'experts' – are men. In this chapter, Gail Young, herself a physician, writes of the contradictions of being a feminist and a doctor.

While writing the chapter, she was a senior houseman (sic) in a northern hospital, and wrote: 'Hopes of a more sane lifestyle when I changed over to maternity last week were shattered by the non-arrival of a new doctor, so we're two instead of four, and every second night on call when you're up half the night is even more crazy. My fury has abated and left me resigned, apathetic and tired. It makes the work very frantic too, with no continuity or time for a chat (except when I'm stitching up!) nor staying with women through labour. I turn up in time to sew them up usually, or if they need forceps or a Caesarian.' Such a description amply demonstrates that the structures within the medical profession and the organisation of the work constrain even those doctors who recognise the need for, and want, change.

Gail Young discusses medical education and training with

particular reference to women doctors. She highlights the difficulties women face in finding expression for 'femaleness' and female values in a profession dominated by men and the 'male' principle of rationality, and suggests that these contradictions operate in such a way as to make it almost impossible to be a 'real' woman doctor.

She looks for solutions in terms of changes in training and education, in terms of a democratisation of the health services, and in terms of encouraging self-help. As she points out, women are the major producers and consumers of health care and it is important for us to use this numerical advantage as a basis for change.

In recent years the male domination of the medical profession has been an object of criticism from feminists. I would like to look at the attitudes among doctors that have provoked this criticism, and at some of the ways in which these attitudes arise and are perpetuated; to explore the experience of women doctors within a male domain, and the experience of people, particularly women, as patients; and to speculate about what changes might give to women (as major providers and consumers of health care) their share in the control of the health services.

The makings of a doctor

Selection for medical school in Britain is at present based mainly on academic results in science 'A' levels or their equivalents, and a high standard is demanded. 'A' levels carry far more weight than personality or suitability to be a doctor, and some medical schools do not even interview candidates. Who your father is, your sporting record, and your social class still carry weight in some London medical schools. This is less so elsewhere, but I would not say that selection is entirely free of class bias. Most medical schools used to have a quota for female entrants, but this has gradually been phased out in the wake of the Sex Discrimination

Act. So the average student entering medical school will be primarily a scientist.

The course in the first few years of medical school perpetuates this emphasis: the volume of work is increased so that there is an overwhelming amount of dry facts to be learned, and teaching is mainly in groups of over a hundred in huge, impersonal lecture halls. The work seems to be only remotely related to looking after ill people. The whole approach to human beings is mechanistic, rationalist and analytical. Creativity and original thinking are easily quashed by the need to remember facts and regurgitate them for frequent exams, failure in which will end one's prospects as a doctor. Already at this stage, medical students tend to stick together, separated from the mainstream of university life by different sorts of pressures and by lack of time.

After two or three years of preclinical science, students emerge cowed and blinking, their critical faculties deadened, ripe for initiation into the mysteries of clinical medicine and, more important, the hierarchical subculture of the teaching hospital. The security of academia and student social life is threatened by confrontation with real ill people, people from totally different backgrounds with different ways of thinking and feeling. Many students find themselves unprepared, feel awkward and ill-equipped in the face of suffering, but, after talking to their patient for the statutory hour, can retreat to the cosiness of theoretical thinking, discuss with their teachers their patient's heart or liver, and compete with fellow students in the detection of obscure physical signs. The contact with patients becomes easier and may soon be enjoyed, found stimulating and broadening, but while a student is expected to know a little about a patient's social background, and to notice if she or he is obviously depressed, these factors are brushed over and the emphasis is still on knowing the symptoms, physical signs, disease processes and the rudiments of treatment.

The main pressures continue to be towards academic success and there is a high degree of competition between students. Women students tend to feel these pressures more strongly and to do better than men academically, perhaps as a result of feeling insecure in a male world, with a sense of a need to prove themselves worthy of the position of honorary man. At the same time there are the usual contradictory pressures on women of having not to appear too clever for fear of threatening the male ego and being sexually undesirable, of being continually up for inspection, and of existing in a masculine sexist milieu. Many women feel confused and feel a separation between their sexual and their academic selves which seem somehow incompatible.

So the foundations are laid for attitudes which are the basis of the hospital subculture. In later years as a clinical student, and especially in the first year after qualification, many doctors feel at a loss for a self-image, because the transition from prolonged adolescence to responsibility is sudden and not well prepared for. The demands made on a newly qualified doctor are very different from those of a comfortable student life. On the first day after qualification the bank manager may allow an overdraft for the first time, but you may also be asked to go and tell a complete stranger that their spouse has died unexpectedly. The house-job year after qualification is an immense strain, partly because of long hours of work, but also because of having real responsibility, prolonged and continuous contact with patients and close involvement with them often for the first time. It is also strange to be treated suddenly with respect and reverence by patients, and to face their expectations of doctors.

Training is not geared to help doctors cope with these realities. Some doctors feel at a loss for behaviour patterns to help them cope with their new position and the emotional strains it entails, and the easy and automatic way out is to model oneself on older doctors who appear to be confident and successful, and to adopt ritual coping behaviour patterns. Apart from the few more mature and sensitive people who survive medical school, or people who from personal experience have a greater understanding of the effects of illness on individuals and families, it seems that the majority of doctors slip easily into this hospital doctor subculture, which provides them with safety and functional role models, and thus perpetuates itself.

The hospital subculture

What are the attributes of this hospital subculture? They include strong pressures towards academic excellence, competitiveness, and one-upmanship games between junior ranks (more prizes for coming up with an interesting quotation from a journal than for knowing how someone is feeling about being ill). This results in doctors who are more interested in *bits* of patients than in *whole* patients, who are more interested in the bits that are fun for them, than the bits that the patient is complaining about, who prefer talking to other doctors than to patients, and who have preconceived ideas about what symptoms patients are supposed to have.

Another factor is the behaviour patterns which help doctors to distance themselves from the potentially horrific emotional strains of actually looking at and seeing the suffering they confront every day, and the pressures of facing up to responsibility. The function of all sentient beings depends on selective perception, the basis for selection being to perceive only information that will contribute to the efficient functioning of the organism. If the definition of efficiency is fairly mechanistic, so will be the perception, and this is the case with hospital doctors. Information which will tend to disturb or threaten a doctor and jeopardise her or his ability to reach a decision quickly and 'rationally' will often be either totally blocked out or distorted.

One of the manifestations of this mechanism is the common habit doctors have of not believing, or diminishing in value, their patients' symptoms. This is especially likely to happen if the patient complains bitterly or to a degree judged by the doctor to be incompatible with the severity of the disease. Doctors like patients who don't complain, even if this leads to disease being left too long, because their demand for relief is less intense and threatens less the doctors' uncertainty about his or her ability to provide relief. Disbelief in symptoms is also likely to occur if the doctor strongly dislikes a patient, sees them often, or is tired when she or he sees them. Very commonly it occurs if the patients have symptoms which the doctor does not understand or cannot rationally explain within the context of the disease models which she or he has learned. These patients are likely to be labelled neurotic or to have their symptoms misinterpreted and to be treated for a condition which the doctor does understand but which they have not got.

Another way in which doctors distort their perception in order to allow themselves to function more efficiently is by depersonalising patients. They are seen as categories or types of people, assessed and classified, put into a mental pigeonhole, and the approach to the patient is based on that classification. According to this classification patients are broadly divisible into acceptable and unacceptable categories. Those who are intelligent, submissive, co-operative and calm, giving clear histories of their disease and having classical symptoms, who have high pain thresholds, and do not demand explanation, are highly acceptable. Patients who are garrulous, emotionally disturbed, demanding, unco-operative, who have low pain thresholds and bizarre symptoms or symptoms which won't go away, and who want detailed explanations, are unacceptable.

This is all encouraged by an attitude to disease which I have already described, and by hospital organisation where patients are seen in an alien environment separated from their own surroundings and in a hurried atmosphere, so that there is no possibility of a deeper understanding. Staff are depersonalised too: by uniform, grade, numbers and institutional life. Doctors work in teams which often fall together in a totally haphazard manner and rarely meet together to get to know each other as people, let alone work out a common philosophy for their medical practice. Work organisation tends to discourage continuity of relationships with other doctors, nurses and patients, and paradoxically those who relate most closely to patients, that is to say nurses and house doctors, have the least power to influence decisions affecting them.

A lot of emotional information is blocked by doctors, both coming from patients and from themselves. There is a degree to which emotional information has to be blocked by everyone but most doctors seem to have a very low tolerance and this is lowered rather than raised by their training.

Emotional symptoms or strong emotions associated with physical symptoms are unacceptable to many doctors, and emotions felt by doctors relating to their patients are even more unacceptable.

The dominant attitude is: 'Don't get involved!' It is permissible to express regret, but not grief, in tragic situations; you are not allowed to react strongly when things happen to your patients or to discuss feelings with other staff. A doctor must remain calm and competent. The demands of genuine open human interaction with patients are felt to be too great and so are rejected.

Tampering with the physiology and psyche of human beings is potentially a very frightening business, especially if the extent of our ignorance, personal or collective, is actually contemplated. Doctors counteract the fear of their own power or powerlessness and their own ignorance by behaving as if they are omnipotent and omniscient. They feel that they remain in control of their patients by doing this; admission of ignorance or helplessness to a patient immediately brings the doctor-patient relationship onto a more equal basis, which makes doctors uncomfortable. Admission of ignorance to other doctors is permissible, preferably to doctors of similar rank, and even then there tends to be embarrassment in the air.

Another way doctors try to maintain their position of apparent omniscience is to monopolise the knowledge they do have, either by refusing to share it altogether, or by couching it in technical language. As Bart and others have pointed out in their chapters, this means that women are often alienated from their own bodies and have no ready access to the information they require on contraception, abortion or childbirth.

Responsibility is felt as a heavy burden by some doctors, and it tends to be borne by individuals rather than shared. In order to remain certain of the rightness of their decisions and to lessen the fear of responsibility, some doctors wall themselves up against criticism, especially criticism or questioning from patients. Many doctors feel afraid that if they have to share decision-making with patients, they will lose an area of control. Responsibility without total control is felt to be unbearable and so doctors defend themselves against sharing. This kind of conflict is increasingly common, especially in obstetrics.

A well-tried and successful way of coping with all sorts of tensions is to divert them into humour, and this is commonly used by doctors. Tales of cardiac arrest scenes where everything went wrong are a common cause for hilarity among junior doctors. There is a tendency too to caricature patients and turn them into comedy figures. Within the hospital, tragedy and comedy are so closely linked that 'You've got to laugh'. This is a feeling which underlies a lot of popular drama and literature about hospitals.

These defence mechanisms commonly used by doctors (that is, denial, depersonalisation, blocking of highly emotional information, self-inflation and punitive behaviour) will obviously adversely affect the doctor-patient relationship. Patients commonly feel that communication is inadequate, that they are not being fully understood or taken seriously, that doctors lack interest and concern, and credit them with very little intelligence and no right to participate in making decisions about their own bodies. To a certain extent, the mechanisms function well in allowing doctors to provide a good standard of physical care, but ultimately the quality of this physical care is affected by poor communication with patients and resistance to criticism. The other problem with these defences is that they are basically evasive and do not allow the individual doctor to confront and experience the stresses fully and thus learn to cope with them directly and thoroughly. Because these defences are never fully successful, more stress is produced, and the doctor becomes even more entrenched in the old behaviour patterns. Thus, the development of the individual's full potential as a human being is prevented and job satisfaction decreased. Once a doctor has reached consultant grade, however, the defences may be found to be functioning quite adequately. The likelihood of developing close relationships with patients is minimal, one is never criticised and always has the final word, and extraordinary degrees of arrogance are tolerated. As the most powerful and respected member of the hospital team, the consultant tends to set the tone for his juniors. These are some of the factors which go to make up the hospital doctor subculture where all medical students and young doctors spend their formative years and I hope it goes some way to explaining why so many doctors seem distant, arrogant, indifferent and patronising, and why the balance of power in the doctor-patient relationship is so unequal.

Women doctors

The hospital doctor subculture in which embryonic doctors develop is basically a male culture. In order to enjoy success within this culture, women doctors have to cultivate male attributes – aggression, competitiveness, rationality, unquestioning self-confidence, emotional coolness. Many doctors, male and female, feel very uncomfortable with the medical subculture, and find a way out as soon as possible, either into general practice where more individualism is allowed, or into a minor speciality. More women do this than men, and obviously the reasons for this are not only that they are misfits culturally, but that, in our society, women still bear the main responsibility for child-rearing and housework, and postgraduate training does not make allowance for this. The paradox is that although it is recognised that women make good doctors, they are seen as incomplete people without marriage and children and, in most cases, motherhood excludes women from higher professional positions. The jobs which have higher proportions of women in them (community health, school medicine, family planning, laboratory-based specialities, radiology, anaesthetics, psychiatry, and part-time hospital sub-consultant posts, or part-time general practice assistantships) are not necessarily in the areas where women have anything particular to offer but where full-time commitment and continuity of care are felt to be less necessary. The areas where perhaps women might have something special to offer, such as obstetrics, gynaecology, paediatrics (empathy and understanding from first-hand experience), and surgery (manual dexterity), are dominated by men. Changes are starting to take place but there is a very long way to go before women doctors will really have equality of opportunity.

There is very little scope for the expression of female attributes in a fulfilling way in working as a doctor. It is difficult to synthesise the woman with the doctor who has emerged from this male culture. In fact, whatever form of home life a woman doctor chooses, whether or not she has sacrificed sex and/or reproduction, she will leave most of her femaleness at home, and if she is in a responsible position, will tend to adopt a masculine stance at work. Women in less responsible or part-time positions may find it easier to be female at work, as they have not been required to cultivate masculine attributes to achieve the position they are in.

However, I would maintain that a woman doctor, whatever her job, is seen in our culture as an honorary man, simply by virtue of society's concept of what a doctor is and what a woman is, and she will therefore have a lot of difficulty in integrating her self-concept as a woman with her doctoring, and in fully expressing herself at work. Men like to see women as submissive, dependent, weak, not too intelligent, highly emotional, and many women accept this view of themselves. People like to see their doctors as rather distant, godlike figures, strong, powerful, clever, and in control of some kind of magic. The images are incompatible. To a certain extent doctors fulfil the need that exists in a patriarchal society, a society based on a religion with a male god and male prophets and saviour, for strong male authority figures, figures whose knowledge and wisdom are unquestioned, who are mysterious, distant, preferably infallible, yet fatherly and caring in a patronising sort of way. Doctors provide a good alternative to the priesthood, also being dabblers in ceremony and ritual, indulging in bizarre initiation rites, and using twentieth-century forms of incomprehensible magic to replace the supernatural sort. A woman in such an archetypal position is unthinkable in our society. A woman's identity as a doctor is therefore uncertain. Many women doctors feel that the word 'doctor' doesn't really apply to them, because of the subconscious masculine stereotype it implies. How far can a woman move outside the classical doctor role and still remain acceptable, or at a certain point will the designation 'doctor' be taken away from her? How far can the barriers of the masculine behaviour patterns that I have described be thrown back without changing the nature of her interaction with patients and other staff so much that she falls off the pedestal they sometimes seem to want her on? Many patients find it difficult to believe that a woman is a doctor especially if she is young, and when this happens a more normal human interaction can take place. There seems to be less difficulty in seeing older women doctors in the classical role, particularly post-menopausal women. This may be something to do with society's view of women's sexuality as diminishing with age: whereas usurping a masculine role is unacceptable in a sexual young woman, it is less unacceptable in an older woman assumed to be less sexual. One's acceptability as a young woman doctor is also related to the power balance that exists in the world outside the consulting room. I have found that relationships with patients can be difficult if the power balance is the complete opposite of what it might be in the street outside. This is mainly true of men between adolescence and late middle age, who are accustomed to being in positions of dominance in relation to younger women. With old men, who are reduced by our society's attitude to old age to a position of relative powerlessness, the relationship becomes more comfortable again.

A woman's discomfort as a doctor is therefore compounded by her difficulty in fitting into the role implied by concepts of what makes a doctor, by her difficulty in finding expression for femaleness at work, and by functioning within a predominantly male culture. For, though the majority of workers in the health service are women, it is undoubtedly the case that it is a male-dominated culture: it is the males who hold the power. The dichotomy between woman and doctor is probably most noticeable in hospital work, and many men doctors also find such work alienating because of the split it imposes between caring and thinking. Doctors (men) think about diseases, nurses (women) care for patients. Promotion tends to distance doctors even further from their patients. The hospital hierarchy puts a woman doctor in a position of power over other women (nurses) who are often older and more experienced and many women doctors find this uncomfortable. Western technological medicine has developed to such a point that enormous power can be wielded over the forces of nature, and besides the fact that women are conditioned into believing that they have no power to wield, using this sort of power demands enormous arrogance and emotional detachment from the patients involved, both of which come hard to women. Obstetrics, for example, is a field where close relationships can develop between women patients and their female attendants. It is an area that has now been technologised, and in which the power has been taken away from the patient and the midwife. Doctors in obstetrics have very little to do with normal births; they intervene when things go wrong. They tend to extend their power by searching out, even creating, the abnormal. The organisation of obstetric 'care' tends actively to discourage continuity and the formation of relationships. All this adds up to frustration for women doctors for whom potentially close relationships with patients are denied, and who find themselves relating to the patient only at the point of intervention in an abnormal labour where their job is to perform painful and unpleasant procedures on the woman and her baby. At other times, decisions may need to be made quickly and clear-headedly without allowing one's concern for the woman involved to cloud matters. These are forms of caring which women find hard in that they are operating a technology invented by men. Similarly, in paediatrics women may find the role of doctor difficult where technological medicine requires the infliction of painful tests and unpleasant treatments on children whom they would rather be comforting.

The dichotomy between woman and doctor is less noticeable in general practice, and many women and men doctors who find hospitals alienating find themselves able to behave as more integrated people in general practice. This is because the relationship between doctor and patient is more intimate, more trusting and more lasting, and because GPs work one-to-one with their patients and are asked to meet very real demands day-to-day, whether 'trivial' or not, whether emotional, social or physical. Many more demands are made on the GP as a human being, and there is less possibility of hiding behind a mythical image or a totally physically-orientated way of thinking. In spite of this, many GPs manage to maintain their distance and their hospital indoctrination, but I think this is an area where there is potential for change in medicine.

So in our culture, being a doctor inevitably involves conflict for a woman. There are practical conflicts with regard to home life and child-rearing, conflicts about being female in a male subculture, conflicts about society's expectations and about her own self-expression. Whatever compromise she chooses, she will have difficulty in synthesising her self-image as a woman with her self-image as a doctor. She may have considerable difficulty in finding a self-image as a woman at all, especially if she chooses not to have a man and children, because all women in our culture are only just beginning to discover what being a woman *is*, apart from attracting men, reproducing and nurturing. Some people might say that the logical conclusion of all this is that women should not be doctors, and many men doctors think this, even if they don't say so openly. I would counter that the doctor's role should change to allow people to be women in it. This means searching for ourselves, our femaleness, beyond the confines of the traditional role, and as we find ourselves, also finding ways of expressing ourselves at work. As a result medicine itself will change, become more female, more wholly human.

How can we change?

The need for change in the medical profession is not yet widely felt from within; rather, there is a solid conservatism and defensiveness in the face of challenges to its power, the expected responses in view of the educational background and learned social defences I have described. Many women doctors have found very satisfactory compromises to deal with the conflicts, by accepting the *status quo* and the need to divide oneself between woman and doctor, and are happy with the satisfactions there are in any sort of doctoring and the privileges it brings.

There is, however, an increasing number of doctors, especially women doctors, who feel uncomfortable with their position and are beginning to criticise articulately from within. As the proportion of women entering medical schools rises towards half, women doctors are recognising the need to push for working conditions and postgraduate training conditions which will allow them, if they wish, to be wives and mothers, without giving up medicine. These are very modest demands in themselves, but at least they are bringing women doctors and medical students together more, and one or two questions are being raised of a more provocative nature, such as the creation of part-time training posts for both women and men, paternity leave, and 24-hour nurseries for children of all health workers. Also, it is being increasingly recognised that the position of women in medicine reflects the position of women in society as a whole; that is, we perform the less popular, less responsible, more routine humdrum jobs with men as our bosses, for less pay, while doing a second job at home, and still express gratitude for the opportunity of participating in public life and earning some money! Parallels are also being noticed between our position and that of the other malleable sector of the workforce, the immigrant doctors, who have been used when needed and whose position is increasingly threatened as the number of British graduates rises.

The majority of health workers are women, and, though they do not present a direct challenge to the power of the medical profession, they have done so indirectly by industrial action which has brought home to doctors how their power to treat patients is dependent on a huge silent infrastructure of menial workers. The *malaise* that exists at present in the NHS offers a great opportunity not only for thinking about its hierarchical structure, but also for women workers (nurses, domestics, radiographers, physiotherapists, and technicians) who provide care as directed by male doctors and administrators, to think about what kind of care they want to provide and whether it is possible within the structure we have.

But what of the consumer of the health services, the

patient? The same subculture, the same social defences, learned by doctors in an attempt to maintain sanity in a stressful job, have for much longer been a source of discontent to patients. The horror stories one hears about contacts with doctors are countless – stories of arrogant doctors who will not listen/won't tell/don't sympathise or who treat people harshly and insensitively – an endless tale of bad communication. Recently this discontent has started to emerge in a more coherent form, and the need for change in the medical profession is increasingly recognised by the public as part of a general move away from uncritical acceptance of authority, directed towards lawyers, religious, political and industrial leaders as well as doctors. Women patients frequently have particular reason for discontent as other chapters show.

For a woman, however healthy, it is almost impossible to avoid contact with the medical profession. Given the nature of the profession this contact is bound to be fraught with difficulty. First, young women seeing doctors are usually basically healthy and healthy women are less likely to accept the imbalance of power which usually exists in the doctor-patient relationship, and which is accepted more easily by people who are ill. Second, the interaction is very often focused on the woman's reproductive organs and her sexuality, and therefore has considerable emotional and personal significance. Third, gynaecology wards, antenatal clinics and obstetric units have an inevitable tendency to be like production lines, by the very nature of the work that is done in them. Doctors tend to have very little understanding of the significance to women of problems related to reproduction and, consequently, there is very little tolerance of the intense emotional reactions that they are bound to meet as gynaecologists. It is recognised by doctors and nurses that gynaecology wards are emotional places but this is safely dealt with by saying 'All gynae patients are mad.' There seems to be a fear of the volcano they are sitting on (which is only a volcano because they are sitting on it) based on the fear of recognising the power of women's sexuality. Women with gynaecological disorders are seen as tainted. If, however, their reproductive organs are functioning in the way deemed good by society, i.e. producing healthy babies, the woman is a heroine, a goddess. It is only recently that serious attempts have been made to understand common 'minor' gynaecological disorders such as pre-menstrual tension and dysmenorrhoea. However, there is still a resistance among doctors to recognise these and other as yet unnamed and unexplained complaints as valid. One wonders how different things would be if men suffered from complaints related to their reproduction and sexuality to such an extent as to need a whole speciality devoted to them. Fourth, most doctors are male, conservative and sexist. As dispensers of fertility control, abortion and obstetric care, they represent the power men have over women's bodies and lives throughout society. As contraception has developed, abortion become legal, and obstetrics technologised, that power has invaded a new area of women's lives. In addition, GPs, psychiatrists and general physicians deal with a lot of unhappiness related to women's position in society and treat it as disease.

It might be interesting to speculate why men end up as obstetricians and gynaecologists. Superficially it would seem that most doctors end up in their particular speciality by a series of accidents of fate and for reasons unconnected with the type of work demanded by patients in that area. Many doctors see obstetrics and gynaecology as attractive because they deal with a younger, healthier population, because they demand a mixture of practical and academic skills, because patients in obstetrics are often happy, and there is wide scope for preventive work and for analysis of the results of treatment policies, and therefore areas for improvement are easily pinpointed. The obstetric work is often seen as compensating for the tedium of gynaecology. A few obstetrician/gynaecologists have a genuine interest in, and concern for, women. A deeper analysis of the motives of obstetrician/gynaecologists in choosing their speciality would be interesting.

Doctors in all specialities, but especially GPs and psychiatrists, find that women take up more of their time than men and that they are confronted with a lot of unhappiness in women presenting itself as a low threshold for complaint in minor illness or as anxiety or depression or sexual problems.

They have failed to relate this to woman's position in society and have treated these problems as disease entities or brushed them off with exasperated comments about the incomprehensibility of women, leaving the individual woman labelled as sick, thus magnifying her own guilt and helplessness.

These are some of the reasons why women find themselves in a position to be critical of the medical profession and why the Women's Movement has emerged as one of the stronger forces of criticism and one of the stronger threads in the self-help movement. Women as the major consumers and providers of health services, are, numerically speaking, in a position to challenge male power.

So what kind of doctors and what kind of doctoring do we want? I would suggest that we want doctors who do not assume they have a right to privilege simply because they are doctors and who see themselves as providing a service rather than bestowing favours; who have a critical awareness of the limitations of Western technological medicine, of its dangers to the patients and of the possibilities of alternative medical disciplines. We need doctors who are capable of sympathy and empathy and of seeing a person as a whole and respecting him or her as an individual; of listening, and taking notice of patients' worries; of feeling and sharing with other health workers their reaction to emotive events and sharing, too, the burden of responsibility.

What kind of changes in training, work organisation, and structure of services could encourage doctors like this to emerge? First of all, the selection of medical students needs to be reviewed. While a certain aptitude in science is necessary, breadth of experience is a greater advantage. More places should be reserved for mature students and active encouragement given to school leavers to spend a year working before going to medical school.

Big changes are needed in undergraduate training. Attempts are already being made at some medical schools to provide courses which give early emphasis to patient-contact, community medicine, and try to integrate the study of the sciences with patient care. Certainly early patient-contact is very important and preferably in a caring role. Perhaps medical students should work as nursing auxiliaries for a while. Science teaching should be seen in the context of its clinical applications. Greater emphasis should be placed on teaching methods of finding and using information rather than the present cramming with superfluous factual detail which will be forgotten. Emphasis should always be laid on thinking of patients as whole people in the context of their family and community, and relating their experiences to one's own experience and life. Creativity should be encouraged by the kinds of tasks set for medical students rather than crushed beneath tomes full of dry facts. In the clinical years of training, time should be found for students to discuss with doctors their feelings about patients and their reactions to their work. Responsibility should be introduced gradually. Competitiveness should be discouraged, and free discussion involving nursing and paramedical staff encouraged. Students should learn how to deal with patients' relatives in a sensitive way.

The provision of a good service would be made easier if postgraduate training laid less emphasis on examination achievement and more on experience and personal qualities. In addition, the organisation of work for junior hospital doctors needs to be looked at. Beyond a certain number of hours per week on duty, the benefit of experience is cancelled out by mental confusion, and patients then suffer. Continuity of care should be encouraged by doctors maintaining responsibility for individual patients throughout the course of their attendance. To further this aim, doctors should adopt the practice of nurses and give each other formal reports on patients at times of duty changeover. Also, time should be allowed for meetings of all health workers involved with patients. Hospital specialists in training should all spend a year in general practice, preferably at an early stage, and GPs should be encouraged to participate in the hospital care of their patients.

In general practice, the doctor-patient ratio is one of the main stumbling blocks to provision of adequate care and this should be reduced as proposed in the new GP charter from around 1:2,500 to 1:1,800. There should be encouragement for GPs to provide more than just basic medical services (for example, counselling and health education) and to encourage patient participation in practice organisation and self-help groups. There should be further encouragement of the team approach to health care which as yet remains a theoretical concept. Health needs to be looked at as a positive attribute rather than the absence of disease and encouraged as such. Team educational activities and regular criticism are needed too.

Throughout the health service more local control is needed, both by health care workers and by consumers, in order to decide locally on health priorities and the organisation of their provision. Women are the main providers of health care at a basic level within and without the health services and we are also the major consumers. Our health care system reflects in its structure, organisation, and philosophy the values of a male-dominated society. Therefore, we as women have a major role in, and responsibility for, challenging the *status quo* from our position as health workers and consumers, and fighting for a health service which is caring and egalitarian, reflects our needs and aspirations as women and the new values which women and feminism can provide.

8

Sex predetermination, artificial insemination and the maintenance of male-dominated culture

Jalna Hanmer

The social control of human biological reproduction takes many forms in our society ranging from technologies designed to affect conception, such as those discussed by Jill Rakusen in relation to Depo-Provera, to the management of birth itself, discussed in Ann Oakley and Hilary Graham's chapter. This chapter explores two innovations, one perfected, artificial insemination, and the other in an experimental stage, sex predetermination. These two were chosen because of the opposing social attitudes held about them and the differences anticipated in their use. They are also likely to inter-connect in an interesting way, since at least in the initial stages, artificial insemination may be necessary for sex predetermination at conception.

Like abortion, contraception and childbirth, artificial insemination and sex predetermination provide a basis for looking at a crucial issue. That is, why are some scientific and technological developments taken up while others are ignored? As science and technology do not play a neutral role in society but respond to the interests of dominant groups, an important question concerns the interests served by a restriction or extension of their use. The preservation and expression of dominant social mores in their present form may depend on the way the technology develops. There may be unintended consequences and, further, individuals may deliberately challenge dominant social mores through their use of sex predetermination and artificial insemination techniques.

Drawing on her own earlier collaborative work on the use of technology (Rose and Hanmer, 1976: Hanmer and Allen, 1980), Jalna Hanmer begins with a brief look at the work on attitudes to sex predetermination and goes on to summarise our understanding of the scientific processes involved in both sex determination (after conception) and sex predetermination (before conception). Passing to the literature on artificial insemination, the author carefully examines both the social comment this has aroused, and the scientific and technological aspects of its use.

The debate is one which has been given little serious attention by feminists so far, but, as Hanmer points out, it is of enormous significance in that it unites theory and practice. On the one hand, women need to look at the meanings of the development of technology in this area. On the other, they need to look at ways of extending their own personal control in much the same way as those women did working in the illegal abortion collective described by Pauline Bart. Such control has been taken by one group of women in Britain, and Hanmer briefly discusses their aims and methods, delineating the threat this poses to male cultural dominance. She discusses how these developments and the state's proposed intervention to extend male control over births currently described as illegitimate is fast becoming a new staging post in the battle for women to control their bodies and their lives.

Women occupy a subordinate position within the family as in society so the question of which sex is conceived if husband and wife differ may become of practical importance. Even if the majority opt for a boy for him first, and girl for her second, the placing within a family affects life chances. First-born children are more likely to achieve academically and socially and even have higher IQ scores than second and subsequent children. A nation of younger sisters does not bode well for women as a group. Fewer women might mean more pressure to marry and to have children, thus reducing even further the control women have over their own bodies and sexuality.

There is a large and growing literature,[1] mainly focused on the USA and the Third World with a little European work, on the attitudes and practices of adults of both sexes, with and without children, to sex predetermination. What is most noticeable about this literature is its volume and the assumption that methods of sex predetermination are likely to be used as soon as they are introduced, although some account is taken of the large number of respondents who express no interest in determining the sex of their children. The work is characterised, on the whole, by a lack of questioning about ethics and morality; rather, one can detect a tendency to cope with possible criticisms by implying or stating that all is not as bad as might be thought. We are told the anticipated swing in the sex ratio in favour of males will right itself after a few years, or that only a minority will care enough to use these techniques.

Respondents are not asked questions that might cast doubt on dominant social values. The questions of social scientists imply that sex predetermination is an accepted and acceptable idea and it is just a matter of finding out which method is preferred, when and how many children are desired, and by which techniques. The rationale for research on sex preferences has been to explore its relation to fertility and thereby its potential contribution to population control. Why people want to determine the sex of their children or why males are thought more desirable are not explored in any depth. The disparity between the preferences of men and women has not been systematically examined although this disparity is one of the major consistent findings. In short, the area is treated as unproblematic.

Unlike sex predetermination, the attention given to artificial insemination by social scientists has been extremely slight, but once again why people feel as they do about what little we know about their preferences remains unexplored. The social comment on artificial insemination is dominated by doctors worried about their legal position, or lawyers' views on this, and the working out of self-imposed rules that maintain dominant cultural values. The lack of attention given to this means of conception by social scientists acts to support dominant ideology regarding the importance of the male to the reproduction of the generations.

To turn to the content of this work, findings indicate that sex predetermination may influence three important population variables: first-child patterns, family size, and the sex ratio (Markle and Nam, 1971). Studies consistently show a preference for a boy for the first child by both men and women. It is believed that family size might be reduced, at least among those who have strong preferences for their children's sex, if the frequent desire for one child of each sex could be met with the first two children. The sex ratio may be further skewed towards males once sex determination is a possibility. Winston (1932), in the first sex choice study in the USA over forty years ago, showed that among his socially superior sample the sex ratio of completed families was 112 boys for every 100 girls (normally expressed as 112:100) compared with a national average of 105.6:100. He suggests that this higher ratio of males to females was achieved through the use of birth control as more couples stopped having children when the child was a boy than a girl (including one-child families), and they were less likely to 'try again' for a girl. His prediction that the extension of birth control throughout the population might lead to an alteration of the sex ratio has not been realised. An explanation is that statistically girls are almost as likely to be born as boys, so continued child bearing to achieve the 'right' number of boys tends to reduce the overall percentages to the normal sex ratio. We do not know if the social class differences he noted in the sex ratio still persist (Clare and Kiser, 1951). Williamson (1976a) points out that there has been little change in attitudes in the USA since Winston's study. She summarises forty years of research on sex preferences of American students by concluding that the preference is for a boy for a first or only child, and for a balanced number of boys and girls if an even number is desired. A preference for a girl as an only child or first child, or for more girls than boys, is rare. Only about one-third of the respondents in the studies she looks at have no preference. The non-student populations studied on the whole favour a smaller increase in male births than does the student population. However, it is difficult to compare studies as questions differ and attitudes vary depending on the situation being considered. For example, the proportion of boys desired rises dramatically if the question asks for a choice on the assumption that only one child is possible. One of the few English studies (Peel, 1970) found that among newly married couples in Hull almost half (46 per cent) wanted one boy and one girl, and some preference in favour of boys emerged as more wanted two boys and one girl (15 per cent) than two girls and one boy (7 per cent). The overall ratio of boys to girls desired was 116:100. The major consistent finding is that men prefer boys more than women do. Ratios can be as high as 165:100 (Winston, 1932). From 66 to 92 per cent of men have been found to want an only child to be a boy (Clare and Kiser, 1951; Dinitz *et al.*, 1954), and from 62 to 80 per cent prefer a first child to be a boy (Markle and Nam, 1971). No study has focused on understanding this major finding although Williamson (1976a) reports that Gini, in a study of European countries, concluded that higher son preference is correlated with higher male status and social position. Winston (1932) suggests that son preference by men is 'natural' and latter-day sociologists may be said to implicitly agree by not treating this consistent finding as one worthy of investigation.

Some studies suggest possible reasons for son preference: for instance, sons carry on the family name, they may be valued for the adults they will become, they offer parents a 'surprise' since what they will become as adults is not preordained and, more immediately, wives wish to please their husbands (Williamson, 1976b; Rent and Rent, 1977). Girls are, therefore, by implication, less valued because they do not carry on the family name, their futures are set as wives and mothers and so they do not bring status or financial rewards into the family or the excitement of variation, and their birth is less likely to please their fathers. Girls may be thought harder to raise or cost more, and the belief that girls should have an older brother may have the status of a moral imperative (Markle and Nam, op. cit.). Fawcett *et al*. (1972, 1974) have suggested that girls are valued for the pleasure they give as children while boys are valued for the adults they will become. Dahlberg (1948) suggests that as most parents want children of both sexes it may be that they are more concerned with the immediate gratification children give. The relative weight and distribution of short- and long-term factors is obscure and these hypotheses largely lack investigation.

Further, no one has concentrated attention on the very low preference for girls, or alternatively, why a minority do prefer girls. For the first child, the choice of a girl is as low as 4 per cent (Dinitz *et al.*, op. cit.; Peterson and Peterson, 1973); for an only child, as low as 15 per cent (Clare and Kiser, op. cit.). While amongst women respondents who want two or four children the resulting sex ratio is close to the actual (105.6:100), for women wanting three, the preference is more often for two boys and one girl (Westoff and Rindfuss, 1974; Rosenzweig and Adelman, 1976). Women not only prefer a male first born but also express more satisfaction with male births generally. Ann Oakley (1978), for example, reports that in her study 54 per cent of the mothers-to-be wanted boys, 22 per cent girls and 25 per cent did not mind, although some of these admitted after the birth that they had in fact wanted a boy. Of those who subsequently had boys, 93 per cent were pleased compared with 56 per cent of those who had girls. Given the higher preference for boys among men we may assume that their husbands were even less satisfied. This raises the question of the impact on the child of being the 'wrong' sex, and particularly the impact on the female child where the experience of not being the 'right' sex is more frequent.

A study by Uddenberg *et al.* (1971) of the sex preferences of women expecting their first child indicates some of the social and personality factors that may be involved. Women wanting sons were found to be more field dependent (i.e.

likely to accede to conventional social demands), indicating immaturity and lack of autonomy, than those wanting daughters or expressing no preference. Field independence was greatest for women desiring daughters with the 'no preference' women in between those choosing daughters or sons. Field independence seems to be associated with being brought up in a family containing boys and girls rather than as an only child or with same sex siblings. While it might be expected that field-independent women would be the more likely to be drawn into the Women's Movement and the experience within it would encourage field independence, another study of a small sample of American women yet to experience pregnancy suggests that women who are strong supporters of the Women's Movement are more likely to prefer sons than women who are not (Rent and Rent, op. cit.).

In the study by Uddenberg *et al.*, a range of mental symptoms were reported both before pregnancy and after the birth somewhat more often among women preferring sons than among those who did not. This result qucstions the Freudian assumption that the birth of a son is the only way a woman can resolve her masculinity complex by compensating her for not being born a man. Further, while analysts have argued that the birth of a girl may intensify mental disturbance, particularly in the woman who is insecure in her feminine role, this study suggests that the birth of a son may be more problematic for a woman's mental health. Among their sample of 81 randomly chosen women with no previous children, 46 per cent wanted boys, 25 per cent girls and 22 per cent expressed no preference. They conclude that it is at least as natural (sic) for a woman to wish for a daughter as a son and that the desire for a son could sometimes be interpreted as an expression of conventionalism. One explanation suggested is that women identify with the expected child and therefore want a child of their own sex. Younger children generally prefer their own sex if asked what they would want for their own baby while older children, presumably in response to cultural conditioning, give preference to male offspring (Hartley *et al.*, 1962).

Williamson (1978) reports that only a few societies

(Singapore, South Korea, Hong Kong and China) have attempted to reduce son preference and then only in efforts to reduce family size. Son preference varies around the world with few societies preferring girls. Of the five societies found which do (the Mudugumor of New Guinea, the Tiwi of North Australia, the Garo of Assam, the Iscobakebu of Peru and the Talowa Indians of north-western California), all are pre-industrial, small-scale groups (one has only twenty-five members). The reasons given for the greater value assigned to daughters are that they are wealth in their own right, hard workers, support their parents in old age, carry on the family line, bring parents a bride-price, can be exchanged for other more valued goods, and produce more daughters. All these societies are matrilineal and only two still exist in the form described in the literature. Yet son preference, while dominant, varies in degree between countries and groups and factors limiting it and encouraging daughter and 'no preference' could be studied.

What *is* universal on the societal level is preference, and if both boys and girls are wanted it is for different reasons. One study puts forward the concept of total family planning (i.e. size, sex of children, birth order, and spacing) arguing that family planning is moving from a negative, contraceptive phase to a positive, proceptive one (Adelman and Rosenzweig, 1978). It is not just that these four characteristics do not exhaust all the possibilities contained in an idea of *total* family planning, e.g. how is conception to occur? Further, the inclusion of sex implicitly conflates the physical reproductive organs (sex) with socially acquired characteristics (gender), negating the importance of social factors. Cultural unisex, i.e. the same gender identity and roles for both sexes, with the accompanying equal individual and social valuation of boys and girls, is a long way off. As women are more likely, and men less likely, to approve of equal valuation and role similarity between men and women, it would seem imperative to focus research interest on these sex-linked differences.

In summary, the literature seems to concern itself largely with the issue of whether sex predetermination will or will not have much effect one way or another on the birth rate. There is argument about the degree of preference, whether or not it will be acted upon, and the importance to be assigned the many variables; for instance, is the general acceptance of the two-child family with the closely associated idea of balance (one of each) more important for the future sex ratio than preferences based on some other number of children (Gray and Morrison, 1974; Thomas, 1951)? After all, we live in a society where son preference is dominant and technology will give individuals the opportunity to express this cultural value more fully, or, alternatively, to challenge it. A new offensive against women may be opening up in the sex war, one that social scientists seem determined to ignore in the pursuit of choice for happy families. But how likely is sex predetermination?

The science and technology of sex predetermination

Desires to influence which sex is conceived and to predict the sex of the foetus once conceived are not only widespread but also of ancient origin. The oldest predictive test is recorded on an Egyptian papyrus around 1300 BC. A bag of wheat and one of barley were moistened daily with the urine of a pregnant woman: if the wheat germinated a boy was predicted, while the germination of the barley foretold a girl. Interpretation of dreams, moods, facial colour, use of and pains on the right or left sides of the body, qualities of breast milk, the activities and positions of the foetus have all been used as indicators along with many others (Cederquist and Fuchs, 1970). Two of the ancient ideas about sex predetermination continue to be the subject of research: the timing of intercourse and the separation of X and Y spermatozoa. In antiquity the latter was attempted by tying up one or the other testicle as the right side was believed to produce boys and the left girls. But prediction and predetermination of the sex of children requires a sounder knowledge of physical processes. It was not until the last decade of the nineteenth century that the role of sex chromosomes was established.

In humans the sex of an individual is controlled by special

chromosomes of which there are two types called X and Y. Each cell has two sex chromosomes and in a woman both these are X chromosomes while a man has one X and a smaller Y. Every ovum (egg) of the woman has one X chromosome while the man's sperm has either an X or a Y. If an X-carrying sperm fertilises the ovum the baby will be a girl, while fertilisation by a Y-carrying sperm produces a boy.

The American gynaecologist Shettles has attempted to popularise a method of sex predetermination that involves the timing of intercourse, douching, coital position and desirability of female orgasm (Rorvik and Shettles, 1977). Knowledge of this method is beginning to percolate through to people who want to try to influence the sex of their child, but key instructions have recently been challenged, opening up a rich area for investigation. Fundamental to methods based on timing of intercourse is knowledge of when conception is likely. No one knows for certain when the ovum is released from the ovary and begins its journey down the fallopian tube to the uterus, or womb, although this is basic to the method. The most reliable indicator that the egg has been, or is about to be, released is the shift in body temperature that takes place on about the fourteenth day of the menstrual cycle. With a rise in progesterone level the body temperature rises a few tenths of a degree and, by keeping a record of daily temperature over three months or so, a graph can be constructed which allows some 80 per cent of women (who ovulate regularly enough) to predict when they are likely to ovulate each month.

Shettles recommended that intercourse should take place on the day before the shift in temperature if a boy was wanted and two or more days before if a girl was desired. Guerrero (1974, 1975) has challenged this advice arguing that the opposite will occur: girls are more likely if intercourse takes place just before the shift and boys if it takes place earlier. Guerrero argues that Shettles's advice is based on the work of Kleegman (1966) in which artificial insemination was the main method used for conception. The advance that Guerrero has made is to show the conflicting trends for natural and artificial insemination. With natural insemination, female conceptions are more likely on the day of the shift and male conceptions in the days before, while the reverse is true for artificial insemination. Artificial insemination usually takes place as close to the day of the shift as possible as this maximises the chance of conception, thus explaining the high ratio of boys born by this method (59.5 per cent male, 40.5 per cent female for more than 10,000 births).

This evidence suggests that the environmental influence of the female reproductive tract may have a differential impact on X- and Y- carrying sperm which affects their survival or fertilising capacity. Guerrero suggests alternative explanations, such as males produce unequal amounts of X- and Y-carrying sperm (Shettles has found evidence of this in a minority of men), or the ovum may allow a differential penetration of the two types of sperm, or one or the other sex does not survive to be implanted in the uterine wall or during early gestation. But these do not explain the differential results between artificial and natural insemination. Little is known about the effect of exposure of semen in the vaginal environment, the role played by sexual excitement, or the mechanisms of sperm transport through the cervix to the fallopian tubes and the ovum.

One factor highlighted by Shettles's advice on douching (a method now regarded as ineffective) is a belief that vaginal acidity favours X-carrying sperm and alkalinity Y-carrying sperm. The vagina is normally acidic and as the temperature shift is approached it becomes more acidic; on the day of the shift, however, the trend is reversed and the vagina becomes more alkaline. The exact opposite phenomenon occurs with the cervix. The view that sexual excitement lubricates the vagina with alkaline fluids, thus favouring male conception, is questioned, although female orgasm as an aid to the conception of male offspring is a belief of ancient standing. The cervical mucus also changes from thick to thin as the temperature shift approaches and this has been suggested as an important factor affecting the progress of the lighter Y- and heavier X-carrying sperm. The assumption that Y-carrying sperm are faster travellers because they are the lighter has not been proved; their relative progress may be determined by the vaginal environment. The commonly expressed metaphor of the process of fertilisation as a race between X- and Y-carrying sperm is questioned as is their sense of direction.

Semen is deposited in the vagina during natural intercourse, and at or in the cervix with artificial insemination as it is thought to make conception more likely. Whether this has any significance for sex ratios has yet to be explored. Guerrero suggests three types of studies are needed: of artificial insemination using the body temperature rise as an indicator of ovulation with single inseminations; clinical studies of the effect of different vaginal environments; and studies of the sex of children conceived as a result of failures of various contraceptive methods which could help to clarify the influence of environmental conditions on sperm.

Not only do we lack the knowledge fundamental to understanding the processes by which each sex is conceived, we also do not understand why the male embryo is less likely to survive until birth. This knowledge gap raises questions concerning the sex ratio. The number of males to females conceived (the primary sex ratio) is not known and estimates vary from 160 or more males for every 100 females to more or less the same ratio as found at birth (Shettles, 1970; Roberts, 1978; Dahlberg, 1951). At birth the ratio is approximately 106 males for every 100 females and this is known as the secondary sex ratio. Why male embryos are more likely to spontaneously abort is not understood. Thus we are left with more questions than answers. Furthermore, clinical trials to test the timing of intercourse founder on the complexity of the instructions.

Two studies have attempted to test Shettles's method: one in Singapore and another in West Germany (Williamson *et al.*, 1978). Both found that only a minority of women became pregnant and of these an even smaller number understood the method well enough and were sufficiently motivated to apply it rigorously. The Singapore study involved an initial contact of 10,000 women of whom 1,000 attended the clinic at least once. Of those with definite sex preferences (all wanted boys) only 31 women attempted to follow the method carefully, and the authors conclude that of these only 6 succeeded in doing so. The results were thus inconclusive. However, Williamson (1978, p. 24) reports that Guerrero's timing schedule is being tested in the UK as well as elsewhere and the Marie Stopes clinic in London is being used as a postal address.

The second potential method for sex predetermination, the separation of X- and Y-carrying sperm followed by artificial insemination, may prove a quicker route to sex predetermination than the timing of intercourse. Sperm separation is possible because the weight of X- and Y-carrying sperm differs. Various methods have been tried: spinning (centrifugation), electrical charge (electrophoresis), and the introduction of substances that encourage filtering of X or Y sperm (selective agglutination). Williamson reports that a method of filtering developed by Ericsson, a physiologist based in California, is being tested in several fertility clinics in the USA, London, Paris and Mexico City, but that few births have taken place so far. Ericsson's method filtrates out Y-bearing sperm only and his plans to market a kit to the medical profession containing the necessary materials for the separation technique have apparently been postponed (Ericsson *et al.*, 1973).[2] Ericsson has patented his technique and started a company named Gametrics Ltd.

Sperm-separating techniques, once perfected, are unlikely to be 100 per cent effective but the odds of conceiving the sex of a child of one's choice will be improved. However, this method involves artifical insemination which will limit its use for practical as well as cultural reasons. Attitude surveys indicate that artificial insemination is a method less favoured than those involving intercourse. The development of pills or a diaphragm that allows one type of sperm to penetrate but not the other, or a special type of prophylactic are all preferred to sperm separation and artificial insemination. Samples of North American students and young married couples indicate that between 15 and 17 per cent either approved or would personally consider using artificial insemination compared with many more (from 46 to 81 per cent) willing to allow others to use a method involving intercourse (Markle and Nam, op cit.; Adelman and Rosenzweig, op. cit.). Questions on the subject's own use produced lower percentages in the study by Adelman and Rosenzweig but still well over half approved of selective intercourse and just below half found a sex-choice pill acceptable, while Markle and Nam found approval of self use to be much lower (26 per cent). Only selective abortion is less favoured as a means of sex selection with responses from 0 to 7 per cent for self use to between 5 and 36 per cent for use by others.

Sex predetermination by sperm separation and artificial insemination is likely to be the first successful method. This technique inevitably will be limited in use given public attitudes and medical involvement. Sex predetermination cannot become routine until a method based on intercourse is perfected and even then it will demand a degree of planning that many couples may find unacceptable. In addition to developing techniques for sex predetermination, the search is on for a safe, accurate means of prenatal sex determination.

Sex determination after conception

If the sex of the foetus could be known before the twelfth week of pregnancy, and if selective abortion on grounds of sex were acceptable, then pregnancy could be terminated by the aspiration method which is safer for the woman and less traumatic than those methods inducing normal labour contractions and birth. The Chinese report that since 1970 they have performed sex determination tests by examining cells along the uterine wall for sex chromatin (Tietung Hospital of Anshan Iron and Steel Company, 1975). Their stated purpose is to help women desiring family planning and, as should be expected, the results of the few cases (100) reported show that many more female foetuses were aborted than male (of the 53 males predicted 1 was aborted, and of the 46 females 29 were aborted). The Chinese report a 94 per cent accuracy with this test performed between the seventh and fourteenth week of pregnancy, but there is some risk of spontaneous abortion. How extensive this type of testing and selective abortion is in China is unknown as are the criteria, if any, for the selection of candidates (for example, any woman or only those with living children?). Two issues are of paramount importance: the governmental acceptance of selective abortion on grounds that the foetal sex is not in agreement with parents' wishes, and the continuing preference for male children among the Chinese.[3]

Western articles stress the value of methods of determining the sex of the foetus for genetic counselling when sex-linked disease is likely rather than for family planning (Goldstein *et al.*, 1973). Sex selection as a form of family planning is not discussed as a serious possibility by scientists in the West, although cautious supporting statements such as 'deserving some consideration' may be found in the literature (Cederquist and Fuchs, op. cit.). Once a safe, reliable, early-detection method is devised, however, we cannot assume that the Western position will not move closer to that of the East, given the continued preference for male children in our society.

The present almost completely reliable method, amniocentesis, has several major drawbacks (Ju *et al.*, 1976). It cannot take place until the sixteenth week of pregnancy and it involves some risks to the foetus, a minimum of three weeks' anxious waiting for the results; it is also an expensive test to carry out. A needle is inserted into the woman's abdomen and a very small amount of amniotic fluid surrounding the foetus is withdrawn for analysis of sex chromatin. The risks, while small, are serious, including puncture of blood vessels or the foetus, the introduction of infection into the amniotic fluid, or premature labour. In Britain, amniocentesis is considered if foetal abnormalities are suspected or sex-linked genetic diseases are known of, and in these situations abortion becomes a possibility.

A number of tests have proved unfruitful; for example, techniques such as staining of mid-cervical smears of pregnant women for the presence of Y chromosomes, hormonal changes in maternal urine, blood and saliva, and a search for possible antibodies that may form in the mother's blood against the male foetus (Shettles, 1971; Goldstein *et al.*, op. cit.; Manuel *et al.*, 1974; Grosset *et al.*, 1974). Research is continuing in this area, however, and it is likely that some method in addition to amniocentesis will eventually be developed.

A partial explanation for the dislike or like of a particular method of sex selection may be described as its visibility and the degree of consciousness its use entails given cultural values about the sanctity of life. Some such explanation is needed to explain why sex predetermination is preferred to determination followed by abortion, and by natural intercourse rather than a method involving a clinical setting and third parties. However, preference for sex predetermination by natural intercourse rather than by artificial insemination involves more than a desire to remain socially, and thus individually, invisible or unconscious.

Artificial insemination

The basis for the cultural resistance to artificial insemination is indicated by the two terms we use to describe it: AIH (artificial insemination by husband) and AID (artificial insemination by donor). Artificial insemination is the introduction of sperm into the vagina by means other than sexual intercourse. The Catholic church is the most opposed to this method of fertilisation, sanctioning neither, while the Anglican position is to accept AIH but not AID. Orthodox Judaism opposes AID and only permits AIH after a number of years without producing children. Most Protestant denominations are either non-committal or oppose AID. Thus, our moral leaders tend to distinguish between the sperm of the husband and that of another. AID is believed to endanger the family, the community, and man (sic) spiritually as it reduces him to the level of the beasts (Emery, 1975; CIBA, 1973). That beasts do not inseminate artificially, except through the hand of man, is not taken into account as the exact truth is irrelevant when major cultural values are threatened.

The knowledge of artificial insemination is of ancient origin, the Talmud (AD 200-250) being the first source. The first recorded human birth was in the latter part of the eighteenth century, although other animals had been artificially inseminated from time to time in earlier centuries. The growth of the practice among domestic animals has expanded rapidly in the last 35 years. In the Western world the major proportion of some livestock, particularly cattle, are conceived in this way. Animals are bred artificially in order to achieve genetic improvement in the stock while in the human artificial insemination is used and justified today as a means of overcoming infertility. One eminent geneticist has argued that artificial insemination should be used to improve the human genetic quality, but this is an unpopular view with its eugenic message and disrespect for marriage, monogamy and 'natural' parenthood (Muller, 1961). Mainstream opinion is more accurately reflected in governmental documents.

The Feversham Committee reported in 1960 (Feversham, 1960).[4] Appointed by the Home Secretary and Secretary of State for Scotland, its terms of reference were to inquire into the practice of artificial insemination, the legal consequences and whether the law should be changed in any way. The Committee distinguished between AIH and AID and recommended that no changes should be made in laws relating to legitimacy or the registration of births. The child conceived by AID is illegitimate as the sperm used is not of the husband. Only the male may confer legitimacy on a child and legitimacy is a question of genetic contribution by a married man to his wife's conception. The Committee was hostile to AID, stating that it should be strongly discouraged but not regulated by law as this would imply a degree of official recognition which would be undesirable. It did not propose that it should become a criminal offence as it was likely the law would be unenforceable. It recommended that conception by AID without the husband's consent should be made a new ground for divorce, but the wife should not have grounds for action if her husband donated sperm without her consent. The Committee expressed unqualified disapproval of artificial insemination of single women. AID was seen as a danger to the institution of marriage. It was criticised for dissociating the responsibility for rearing children from their procreation (a point which in fact applies only to men). The selection of suitable couples for AID was seen as problematic given a belief in the need for full investigation into psychological and family background factors.

The practice of AID, however, has continued to grow

slowly as knowledge of this means of alleviating some forms of infertility has spread among the public and as attitudes have slowly become more favourable (Brudenell *et al.*, 1976).

In 1971 the British Medical Association set up a panel which looked at the medical, ethical and legal aspects of AID (BMA, 1973). While they felt that there was a very real danger of too ready a resort to AID, particularly given the relatively easy nature of the procedure, they recommended that it be offered by the National Health Service and that frozen semen banks be set up.[5] The legal position of doctors is not clear although it is thought that the law of negligence applies in the same way to this procedure as to any other medical treatment. There is no way to ensure that all the sperm used in the insemination are genetically sound and the possibility of birth anomalies exist in the same proportion among women inseminated artificially as through intercourse. This is not the only situation possibly involving litigation and doctors are advised to gain the written consent of husband and wife even though this may not be a full defence.

The British Medical Association panel recommended that the minority report of the Feversham Committee be adopted. This would extend the definition of legitimacy to include a child born as a result of AID if the husband consented, and that the mother's husband should be taken as the father of the child for purposes of registration of birth. As it is widely assumed that husbands are illegally registering as the fathers of children conceived by AID, this change would bring the law into line with actual behaviour.

In law the child of a married woman is presumed to be that of the husband as long as 'he is within the four seas'. Given the confidential nature of AID there is no difficulty in the husband being accepted without question as the father of an AID child when the birth is registered. Adoption, the other way to legitimate a child, is seen as too cumbersome a procedure given the ease with which the present law can be evaded. The 1979 report of the Law Commission recommends that these changes be endorsed by parliamentary action.[6] As fatherhood is legally held to reside in the genetic contribution, the acceptance of AID children as legitimate is a break with a particularly ancient tradition, one at the very root of patriarchial social orders. It is worth reflecting on why this departure must now be made. To do so means looking briefly at the central issue of concern to the Law Commission: the extension of rights to men over children presently deemed illegitimate.

Some 10 per cent of children are illegitimate under the present law and, while this is not the first time this figure has been reached in Britain, after a decline it is again on the increase. If the envisaged changes to the law are adopted, fathers will gain rights of custody, guardianship and access whether married or not to the child's mother. It seems that now the stigma of bastardy is declining new legislation is needed in order to retain men's rights over women and children. Possibly there will even be an extension of male rights as these changes might function to support a form of polygyny. What is to stop men having control over a number of children by different women (and in this way to gain control over the women)? Men will gain these rights to the child if the mother gives his name when the birth is registered, if he signs the birth certificate or if a court finds that he is the father. The mother will have to prove that the man is not the father rather than the father establishing his paternity, and living with her, for example, is likely to be sufficient to establish his claim.

Several months before the Law Commission reported, the House of Lords discussed a bill put forward by James White (1978) calling for similar legal changes. During the course of the debate, the government spokesman pointed out that many women may be unhappy about the extension of rights to men who may play little role in the care of the child and recognised that this change would mean the taking of rights from women. Mothers at present have undisputed guardianship and custody of their illegitimate children and the fathers have no right of access. Women's Aid[7] has exposed the particularly poor situation the married woman finds herself in compared with that of the cohabiting woman in violent matrimonial situations. Every year, deaths of married women result from access to children required by law; threats of contested custody cases cost women untold agony and threat to their persons, as the obligatory court appearances enable men to locate 'their' women. The woman with illegitimate children faces none of these harassments.

While the Law Commisison speaks of responsibilities as well as rights, by which they largely mean financial contribution to the maintenance of the child, the Finer Committee (1974) on one-parent families has conclusively documented the true state of affairs. Few men need pay a penny towards the upkeep of their children if they do not wish to do so. A man's assumption of responsibility towards his children is almost purely voluntary. We are likely to be entering a period when it will be progressively harder for women to have children without a man having considerable hold and control over them both. This poses a crucial question. Is the child the desired object of this proposed legislation or is the woman? Whatever the answer, the proposals of the Law Commission will put both into the control of men thus affecting all but the most resolute of women.

And such resolute women do exist. Women are beginning to meet together in groups and, with the help of willing men, inseminate themselves, deliberately bearing bastards. Events have moved beyond the occasional lesbian couple who wish a child; the scandal of yesterday. Why cannot women legitimate their children? After all, every child can be identified easily through its biological relationship with its mother. This question is of core significance in a patriarchal social order for both those who wish to destroy it and for those who wish to find ways of maintaining existing relations of power in changing circumstances.[8]

Artificial insemination has the potential for acts of rebellion. Artificial insemination is a simple procedure which requires neither a clinical setting nor a doctor. Yet artificial insemination is not as fully understood as clinicians would like (Jones, 1971). A major difficulty is the absence of criteria for predicting the fertility of a sample of semen. Physical activity and number of sperm per milligram are the most frequently used indicators. While medical students and other health personnel are often used as donors given their accessibility, arguments are made for selecting men with two or more healthy children as their capacity to produce viable sperm is proven. It is not possible to compare the success rates of different studies given the variation in crucial variables (i.e. the women's fertility, the method of determining ovulation, the different types and number of inseminations used, and the quality of semen). However, when all cases are aggregated success rates of 60-75 per cent are obtained with fresh donor semen. Frozen donor semen results are lower, from 40-55 per cent (Emery, op. cit.).

Frozen semen allows easier access; it is available when needed. Its value in livestock production is obvious and frozen sperm banks are also needed for artificial insemination to expand among humans. The reasons why frozen semen is less efficient than fresh are not understood. Human insemination with frozen semen has been achieved after several years but the total number of pregnancies achieved from semen stored longer than six months has been very small. Insemination with fresh or frozen semen does not increase the proportion of spontaneous abortion and miscarriage, tubal pregnancies or birth anomalies found in pregnancies resulting from intercourse. More inseminations have taken place with fresh semen and the final weighing up of the differential results to be obtained with fresh or frozen has yet to be made. One difference noted, however, is in the sex ratio. Of more than 10,000 births, fresh semen produced 59.5 per cent male and 41.5 per cent female while frozen semen resulted in 45.1 per cent male and 54.9 per cent female.

Clinicians vary in their insemination technique. Insemination can vary from once to six times per cycle and the inseminate may be placed in the vagina, the cervix or the uterus. A cervical cap may be used to keep the semen in place. On average it takes four months and six inseminations to achieve pregnancy with fresh donor semen and five months and seven inseminations with frozen. The women described above who have been meeting for self-insemination use the following procedure. They work out their likely time of ovulation by temperature charts and cervical mucus changes – in the same way as for the rhythm method of contraception. At the time of ovulation and using semen from a group of homosexual men, they draw the sperm into a needleless syringe and put it into their vaginas, usually lying down for half an hour or so afterwards.

The women spoken to are doing this because, as lesbians, they do not want to have sex with a man merely in order to get pregnant. Inseminating themselves, they say, 'seems much more "right" for us because we are in control of the means and the experience'. For these women, self-insemination is an important part of their political struggle since it separates reproduction from sexual enjoyment, allowing women the ability to choose to have a child while both men and women have the freedom to develop the sexual relationship of their choice.

This activity flies in the face of conventional wisdom with its patriarchal value structure. Some clinicians do extensive tests to establish the woman's fertility before they consider the question of the husband's infertility and artificial insemination, which shows the strength of cultural belief that the reproductive capacity of the woman is the husband's private property. Other clinicians try artificial insemination sooner and only resort to all the tests if the woman does not become pregnant after three or four months. The literature recommends that the couple go through a rigorous selection procedure involving scrutiny of their marriage, their personalities and their motivation. It is believed to be essential that the donor is anonymous, which is obviously important if the reproductive capacity and product of the woman can be acquired as private property by men.

To conclude, sex determination by amniocentesis is of proven success and, when linked with selective abortion, could be a means of sex predetermination, but it is only the Chinese who claim to use this type of combination. Methods involving the timing of intercourse are being, and have been, monitored. State involvement was direct in Singapore, but is indirect in the West. If state funding is being used in the current trials in the West it is probably because the personnel involved are working in state funded hospitals and laboratories. It may appear a non-contentious activity to all concerned as clients seek out medical workers willing to advise and monitor results. The myth of value-free science is maintained by the apparent lack of connection between institutions in receipt of state funding and the individuals who work within them. The myth is that scientists do what they want, following their 'hunches' etc. without interference, or respond to human 'need'; there is no issue of resources and their use in a value-free scenario.

A comparison of sex predetermination and artificial insemination allows us to see clearly the patriarchal culture in the act, albeit unconsciously, of self-maintenance. Sex predetermination is no threat to male dominance; hence, no obstacle is anticipated in its use other than the time it takes for people to grow accustomed to something new (which will happen, it is said, as more and more use it). Sex predetermination is unlikely to change the patriarchal emphasis of our society but, adopted on a wide-scale, and this depends on the technique developed, it offers the possibility of strengthening son preference and daughter non-preference, of reinforcing sex roles by under-writing the conflation of sex and gender, of altering the sex ratio further in favour of males, of placing greater restriction on women's limited control over their reproductive capacities.[9]

Artificial insemination by donor, however, is more problematic, hence its slow growth and the necessity for the state to grapple with its potential for freeing women from the patriarchal family structure where women and children are largely controlled by the male, and where the wife role keeps women out of the labour market as serious competitors to men and their much greater earnings. Women on their own with children who have no known father do threaten the family, the community and men, as our moral leaders clearly recognise. We can expect the state to act through legislation in an effort to maintain male dominance. The simplicity of the technique, however, makes it impossible to restrict artificial insemination to use by professionals. This technique may serve a woman's right to choose when, where and how to produce children (as may sex predetermination for field-independent women), but it is unlikely to become a major means of conception as it offers no benefit to male cultural dominance.

In these ways a child's sex and means of conception are in the process of becoming a new battleground in the running war between the sexes.

Notes

1 For a summary and excellent bibliography of the work on sex preferences, see Williamson (1976a).
2 The separation of X-carrying sperm has been claimed by Adimoelia *et al.* (1977). See also Shastry, Hegde and Rao (1977).
3 The Chinese, according to an article in *People* (1979, 6:2, pp. 17-20), encourage two-child families except when both children are female or if a child has a birth defect.
4 For comment on the Feversham Committee, see *The Lancet*, 30 July 1960, pp. 247-8, and *British Medical Journal*, 30 July 1960, pp. 379-80.
5 A service of this type has been offered by the British Pregnancy Advisory Service since 1979.
6 This legislation is anticipated by the British adoption of the European Convention on the Legal Status of Children Born out of Wedlock, Council of Europe, 1975, Strasbourg.
7 The National Women's Aid Federation has over 100 member groups providing refuge to women escaping violent marriages.
8 Mary O'Brien (1979) answers this question by arguing that the male appropriation of the child mediates the opposition between *his* exclusion from genetic continuity (reproduction begins with the alienation of the male sperm) and social recognition as a father, and *her* experience of genetic continuity (paternity is largely an idea while maternity is an experience). This opposition generates a dialectical process necessitating co-operative action between men to achieve 'rights' to the child, a social, legal and political process. O'Brien argues that as with any material dialectical process changes occur over time and thus far we have witnessed two: the discovery of the male role in reproduction and developments in contraception. Further developments in reproductive engineering, particularly the artificial placenta, will offer the same discontinuous experience to women as men now have. This could be another way to resolve the present opposition and offer explanation for why men want these developments.
9 Williamson (1976b), less pessimistically, argues that woman may benefit from sex predetermination, as it may give women more control over their bodies and their lives. My own view is that the opposite is more likely and the vision of the biologist Postgate (1973) is instructive. He sees women's reproductive and sexual servicing roles as becoming dominant as their proportionate numbers decrease, and describes women as queen bees to be given as rewards to outstanding males. We therefore need to consider how daughter preference can be increased.

References

Adelman, S. and Rosenzweig, S. (1978), 'Parental Predetermination of the Sex of Offspring: II The Attitudes of Young Married Couples with High School and with College Education', *Journal of Biosocial Science*, vol. 10, pp. 235-47.

Adimoelia, A., Hariadi, R., Amitaba, I. G. B., Adisetya, P. and Soeharno (1977), 'The Separation of X and Y Spermatozoa with Regard to the Possible Clinical Application by Means of Artificial Insemination', *Andrologia*, vol. 9, no. 3, pp. 289-92.

British Medical Association (1973), 'Report of Panel on Human Artificial Insemination', *British Medical Journal Supplement*, vol. 2, no. 2, pp. 3-5.

Brudenell, M., McLaren, A., Short, R. and Symonds, M. (eds) (1976), *Artificial Insemination*, Proceedings of the Fourth Study Group of the Royal College of Obstetricians and Gynaecologists.

Cederquist, L. L. and Fuchs, F. (1970), 'Antenatal Sex Determination: A Historical Review', *Clinical Obstetrics and Gynaecology*, vol. 13, pp. 159-77.

CIBA Foundation Symposium 17 (1973), *Law and Ethics of A.I.D. and Embryo Transfer*, Elsevier, Excerpta Medica, North Holland.

Clare, J. E. and Kiser, C. V. (1951), 'Social and Psychological Factors Affecting Fertility', *Millbank Memorial Fund Quarterly*, vol. 29, no. 1, pp. 440-83.

Dahlberg, C. L. (1948), 'Do Parents Want Boys or Girls?', *Acta Genetica*, vol. 1, no. 2, pp. 163-7.

Dahlberg, G. (1951), 'The Primary Sex Ratio and its Ratio at Birth', *Acta Genetica et Statistica Medica*, vol. 2, no. 3, pp. 245-51.

Dinitz, S., Dynes, D. and Clarke, A. (1954), 'Preferences for Male or Female Children: Traditional or Affectional?', *Marriage and Family Living*, vol. 16, pp. 128-30.

Emery, A. E. H. (ed.) (1975), *Modern Trends in Human Genetics*, Butterworth, London.

Ericsson, R. J., Langevin, C. N. and Nishino, M. (1973), 'Isolation of Fractions Rich in Human Y Sperm', *Nature*, no. 246, pp. 421-4.

Fawcett, J. T., Albores, S. and Arnold, F. (1972), 'The Value of Children Among Ethnic Groups in Hawaii: Exploratory Measurements', in J. T. Fawcett (ed.), *The Satisfaction and Costs of Children: Theories, Concepts, Methods*, East-West Population Institute, Honolulu, Hawaii.

Fawcett, J. T., Arnold, F., Bulatao, R. A., Buripakdi, C., Chung, B. J., Iritani, T., Lee, S. J. and Wu, T. S. (1974), 'The Value of Children in Asia and the United States: Comparative Perspectives', paper of the East-West Population Institute, Honolulu, Hawaii.

Feversham Committee (1960), *The Report of the Departmental Committee on Human Artificial Insemination*, Cmnd. 1105, HMSO, London.

Finer Committee (1974), *Royal Commission on One-Parent Families*, vols. I and II, Cmnd. 5629, HMSO, London.

Goldstein, A., Lukesh, R. and Ketchum, M. (1973), 'Prenatal Sex Determination by Fluorescent Staining of the Cervical Smear for the Presence of a Y Chromosome: An Evaluation', *American Journal of Obstetrics and Gynaecology*, vol. 115, p. 866.

Gray, E. and Morrison, M. (1974), 'Influence of Combinations of Sexes of Children on Family Size', *The Journal of Heredity*, vol. 65, pp. 169-74.

Grosset, L., Barelet, V. and Odartchenko, N. (1974), 'Antenatal Foetal Sex Determination from Maternal Blood During Early Pregnancy', *American Journal of Obstetrics and Gynaecology*, vol. 120, no. 1, pp. 60-3.

Guerrero, R. (1974), 'Association of the Type and Time of Insemination within the Menstrual Cycle and the Human Sex Ratio at Birth', *The New England Journal of Medicine*, vol. 291, pp. 1056-9.

Guerrero, R. (1975), 'Type and Time of Insemination within the Menstrual Cycle and the Human Sex Ratio at Birth', *Studies in Family Planning*, vol. 6, no. 10, pp. 367-71.

Hanmer, J. and Allen, P. (1980), 'Reproductive Engineering – The Final Solution?', in L. Birke and S. Best, *Alice Through the Microscope: The Power of Science Over Women's Lives*, Virago, London.

Hartley, R., Hardesty, F. P. and Gorfein, D. S. (1962), 'Children's Perceptions and Expressions of Sex Preference', *Child Development*, vol. 33, p. 221.

Jones, R. C. (1971), 'Uses of Artificial Insemination', *Nature*, vol. 229, pp. 534-7.

Ju, K. S., Park, I. J., Jones, H. W. and Winn, K. J. (1976), 'Prenatal Sex Determination by Observation of the X and Y Chromatin of Exfoliated Amniotic Fluid Cells', *Obstetrics and Gynaecology*, vol. 47, no. 3, pp. 287-90.

Kleegman, S. J. (1966), 'Can Sex be Predetermined by the Physician?', *Excerpta Medica*, vol. 109, p. 109.

Law Commission Working Paper 74 (1979), *Family Law and Illegitimacy*, HMSO, London.

Manuel, M., Park, I. J. and Jones, H. W. (1974), 'Prenatal Sex Determination by Fluorescent Staining of Cells for Prêsence of Y Chromatin', *American Journal of Obstetrics and Gynaecology*, vol. 119, pp. 853-4.

Markle, G. E. and Nam, C. G. (1971), 'Sex Predetermination: Its Impact On Fertility', *Social Biology*, vol. 18, no. 1, pp. 73-83.

Muller, H. J. (1961), 'Human Evolution by Voluntary Choice of Germ Plasm', *Science*, vol. 134, no. 3480, pp. 643-9.

Oakley, A. (1978), 'What Makes Girls Differ from Boys?', *New Society*, 21 December, pp. xii-xiv.

O'Brien, M. (1979), 'The Politics of Reproduction', in M. K. Shirley and R.E. Vigler, *In Search of the Feminist Perspective: the Changing*

Potency of Women, Ontario Institute for Studies in Education, Toronto.

Peel, J. (1970), 'The Hull Family Survey 1. The Survey of Couples, 1966, *Journal of Biosocial Science*, vol. 2, pp. 45-70.

Peterson, C. C. and Peterson, J. L. (1973), 'Preference for Sex of Off-spring as a Measure of Change in Sex Attitudes', *Psychology*, vol. 10, pp. 3-5.

Postgate, J. (1973), 'Bat's Chance in Hell', *New Scientist*, 5 April, pp. 12-16.

Rent, C. S. and Rent, G. S. (1977), 'More on Offspring-Sex Preference: A Comment on Nancy E. Williamson's Sex Preferences, Sex Control, and the Status of Women', *Signs*, vol. 3, no. 2, pp. 505-15.

Richardson, D. W. (1975), 'Artificial Insemination in the Human Secondary Sex Ratio', *Journal of Biosocial Science*, vol. 10, pp. 169-82.

Roberts, A. M. (1978), 'The Origins of Fluctuations in the Human Secondary Sex Ratio', *Journal of Biosocial Science*, vol. 10, pp. 169-82.

Rorvik, D. and Shettles, L. (1977), *Choose Your Baby's Sex*, Dodd, Mead, New York.

Rose, H. and Hanmer, J. (1976), 'Women's Liberation, Reproduction and the Technological Fix', in D. Barker and S. Allen, *Sexual Divisions and Society: Process and Change*, Tavistock, London.

Rosenzweig, S. and Adelman, S. (1976), 'Parental Predetermination of the Sex of Offspring: The Attitudes of Young Married Couples with University Education', *Journal of Biosocial Science*, vol. 8, pp. 335-46.

Shastry, Hegde and Rao (1977), 'Use of Ficoll-Sodium Metrizoate Density Gradient to Separate Human X and Y Bearing Spermatozoa', *Nature*, vol. 269, p. 58.

Shettles, L. B. (1970), 'Factors Influencing Sex Ratios', *International Journal of Gynaecology and Obstetrics*, vol. 8, no. 5, pp. 643-7.

Shettles, L. B. (1971), 'Use of the Y Chromosome in Pre-natal Sex Determination', *Nature*, vol. 230, p. 52.

Thomas, M. H. (1951), 'Sex Pattern and Size of Family', *British Medical Journal*, vol. 1, pp. 733-4.

Tietung Hospital of Anshan Iron and Steel Company, Anshan (1975), 'Foetal Sex Prediction by Sex Chromatin of Chorionic Villi Cells During Early Pregnancy', *Chinese Medical Journal*, vol. 1, no. 2, pp. 116-26.

Uddenberg, N., Almgren, P. E. and Nilsson, A. (1971), 'Preference for Sex of the Child Among Pregnant Women', *Journal of Biosocial Science*, vol. 3, pp. 267-80.

Westoff, C. F. and Rindfuss, R. R. (1974), 'Sex Preselection in the United States: Some Implications', *Science*, vol. 84, no. 4137, pp. 633-6.

White, J. *et al.* (1978), 'A Bill to Remove the Legal Disabilities of Children Born out of Wedlock', 29 November HMSO; discussion of the 'Children Bill', on 23 February 1979, *Hansard*, pp. 807-45.
Williamson, N. E. (1976a), *Sons or Daughters: A Cross-Cultural Survey of Parental Preferences*, vol. 31, Sage, Beverly Hills.
Williamson, N. E. (1976b), 'Sex Preferences, Sex Control and the Status of Women', *Signs*, vol. 1, no. 4, pp. 847-62.
Williamson, N. E. (1978), 'Boys or Girls? Parents' Preferences and Sex Control', *Population Bulletin*, vol. 33, no. 1.
Williamson, N. E., Lean, T. H. and Vengadasalam, D. (1978), 'Evaluation of an Unsuccessful Sex Preselection Clinic in Singapore', *Journal of Biosocial Science*, vol. 10, pp. 375-88.
Winston, S. (1932), 'Birth Control and the Sex Ratio at Birth', *American Journal of Sociology*, vol. 38, no. 2, pp. 225-31.

Index